RESPONSIBLE TRAVEL GUIDE

Cambodia

Improving Lives Through
Thoughtful Travel Choices

by

Pujita Nanette Mayeda

and

Friendship with Cambodia

Wild Iris Press
Eugene, Oregon

Responsible Travel Guide Cambodia
by Pujita Nanette Mayeda and Friendship with Cambodia
published by Wild Iris Press

Contributing Writers
Kathie Carpenter, Lowell Hill, Shoshana Kerewsky, Carol Pucci,
Bhavia Wagner, ConCERT, Cornell University Southeast Asia Program

Acknowledgements
My deepest gratitude goes out to Shigeo Takayama for his support in funding this project,
Tom Auciello for his superb map-making skills, Bhavia Wagner for her generosity,
Matthew Reese, Solala Towler and Jackie Van Rysselberghe for their astute editing and
my dear family & friends for their continuous love and support.

Friendship with Cambodia
PO Box 5231, Eugene OR 97405 USA
info@friendshipwithcambodia.com
www.friendshipwithcambodia.org

ISBN 978-0-9753951-1-0

Printed in the United States of America & the United Kingdom

This book is lovingly dedicated to
Mata Amritanandamayi
for her inspiration, selfless service,
humanitarian projects and
unconditional love.

CONTENTS

How This Book Came About

When I first visited Cambodia in 1991, tourists were not allowed to enter the country. Cambodia was ruled by a Vietnamese-backed communist government. To get us across the border, our driver had to make up a story and said that we were health-care workers.

I spent a week in Phnom Penh – it was eerie, like a ghost town. The streets were empty, except for a few cargo trucks. The only hotel was the Le Royal. It smelled like a sewer and bats were flying down the hallways. Curious children, standing warily at a distance, were barefoot and dressed in rags. The market vendors had blank looks, still in a state of shock from the genocide they had experienced 12 years earlier.

Today, Cambodia presents a very different face. The streets are packed with cars and motorbikes. The tourist industry is booming, with hotels and restaurants to suit everyone's taste and budget. The Cambodians you meet have warm smiles and are kind and helpful.

But if you chat with your driver or guide about his life, you learn that some or even all of his family members died in the genocide. You are at a loss for words… "Why did that happen?" you ask. "I don't know," comes the honest answer. Most Cambodians over 30 years old experience various forms of post traumatic stress, many having frequent nightmares from the terror of the killing fields.

From the window of your taxi, things look pretty good, but if you spend some time in the rural areas, where 85% of Cambodians live, you will find that almost half of the children are malnourished and two-thirds of the population do not have clean drinking water. Poverty forces seventy-five percent of the children to drop out of grade school. Their parents, who earn an average of $1 a day, cannot afford school clothes, books or fees.

What can you do? You are on vacation. You want to have a good time. Yet the poverty tugs on your conscience, like the children begging you to buy a postcard.

I didn't know what to do. But I felt drawn to return. The following year I went back to Cambodia and searched out non-profit groups helping women. I offered to help sell their handicrafts in the United States. This time there was a feeling of hope in the air, because the communists had left and the United Nations had arrived in their shiny white trucks to help orchestrate a national election. Most Cambodians knew nothing about democracy, but they were about to get a crash course.

Something in Cambodia kept pulling me back. There was real heroism here – in spite of all the tragedy these people experienced, I found that they were positive and kind. They were working hard to rebuild their shattered country. Every Buddhist temple had been destroyed by the Khmer Rouge and yet most of them were being rebuilt. I started leading tours to Cambodia for Global Exchange and sought out ways to help people.

I discovered really nice hotels and restaurants that were training programs for disadvantaged youth. I found craft shops run by organizations that were helping landmine survivors and families with AIDS.

What kept bothering me was that the shops were often empty, even when the streets were packed with tour buses. That is what gave me the inspiration for this book: to let people know how they can help the poor in Cambodia and have fun at the same time!

It was a good idea, but I had started Friendship with Cambodia, a non profit organization that supports humanitarian projects and that took all my time. So when Pujita Mayeda offered to work on the book as a volunteer, I felt as though an angel had arrived. She spent endless hours doing research and made a trip to Cambodia on her own dime to visit most of the businesses listed in this book.

With help from several other talented volunteers from Friendship with Cambodia, she has pulled together this very fine guide for how to visit Cambodia in a way that helps local people and the environment. Even if you just purchase this book you will help people in Cambodia because the profits support our humanitarian work.

I invite you to delve into this guidebook and enjoy visiting Cambodia. When you return home you will feel good because you did not just take, you gave something back.

Bhavia Wagner
Executive Director
Friendship with Cambodia

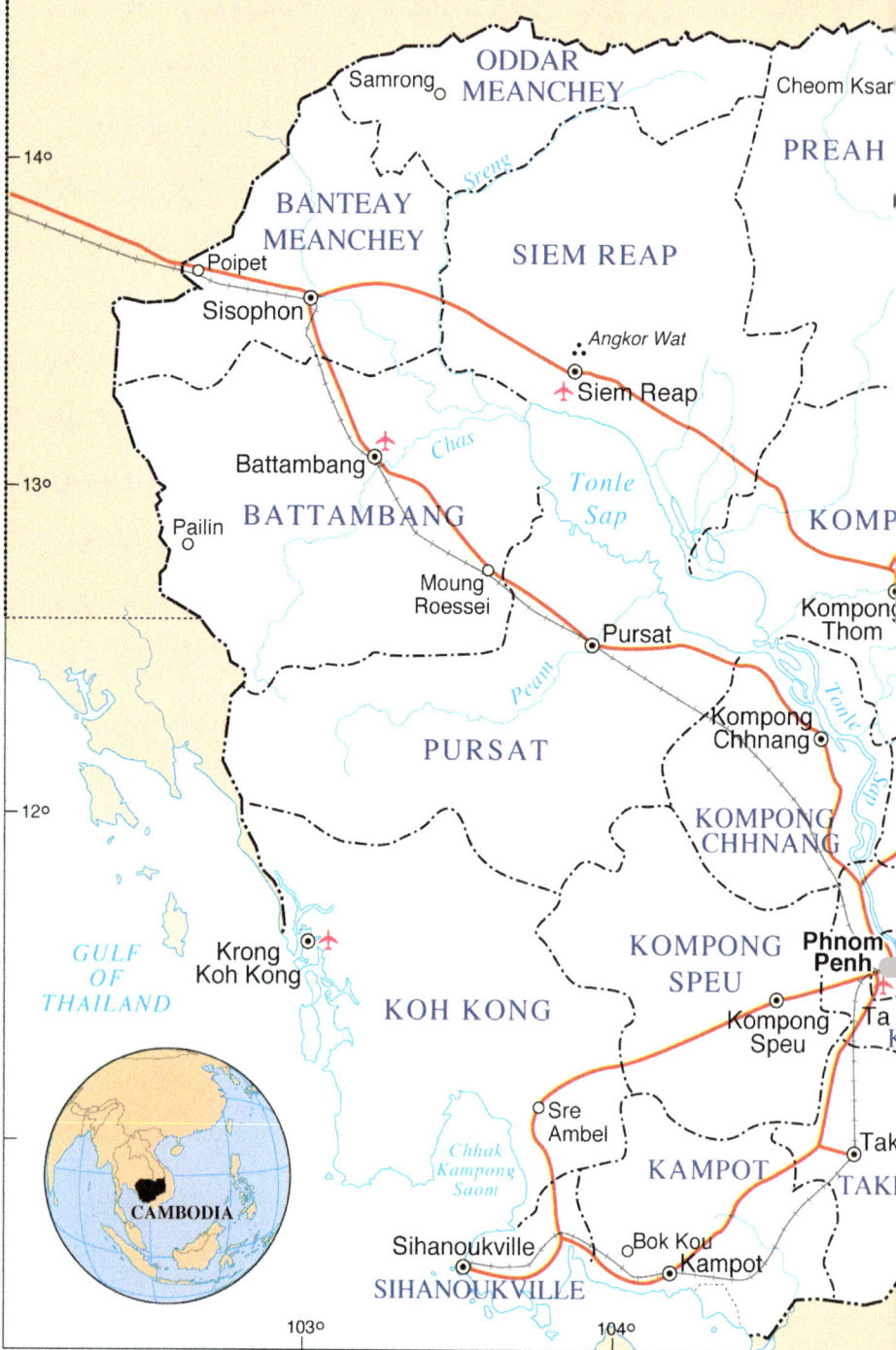

CAMBODIA

THAILAND

104°

ODDAR
MEANCHEY

Samrong

Cheom Ksar

PREAH

14°

Sreng

BANTEAY
MEANCHEY

SIEM REAP

Poipet

Sisophon

Angkor Wat

Siem Reap

Battambang

Chas

*Tonle
Sap*

KOMP

13°

Pailin

BATTAMBANG

Kompong
Thom

Moung
Roessei

Pursat

Pean

KOMPONG
CHHNANG

Kompong
Chhnang

Tonle

PURSAT

12°

GULF
OF
THAILAND

Krong
Koh Kong

KOMPONG
SPEU

**Phnom
Penh**

Kompong
Speu

Ta
k

KOH KONG

Sre
Ambel

*Chhak
Kampong
Saom*

Tak

KAMPOT

TAK

CAMBODIA

Sihanoukville

Bok Kou
Kampot

SIHANOUKVILLE

103°

104°

LAO PEOPLE'S DEMOCRATIC REPUBLIC

VIHEAR

Siempang

STUNG
TRENG

RATANAKIRI

Phnom Thbeng
Meanchey

Boung Long

Stung Treng

Lumphat

Kong

San

Mekong

PONG THOM

Sen

KRATIE

MONDOL
KIRI

Chinir

Kratie

Senmonorom

KOMPONG CHAM

Snoul

Kompong Cham

VIETNAM

Mekong

Prey
Veng

PREY
VENG

Khmau
KANDAL

Banam

SVAY
RIENG

Bassak

keo

KEO

Svay Rieng

✪	National capital
◉	Provincial capital
○	Town, village
✈	Major airport
–·–··–	International boundary
–·–·–	Provincial boundary
—	Road
+++	Railroad

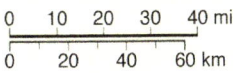

0   10   20   30   40 mi

0   20   40   60 km

105°   106°   107°

14°

13°

12°

105°

Divinely beautiful Apsaras grace the temples of Angkor Wat.

Sihanoukville beaches invite rest for weary travelers.

Rewarding volunteer opportunities lead to classroom journeys with Cambodia youth.

*Hopeful enthusiasm
of Cambodian youth.*

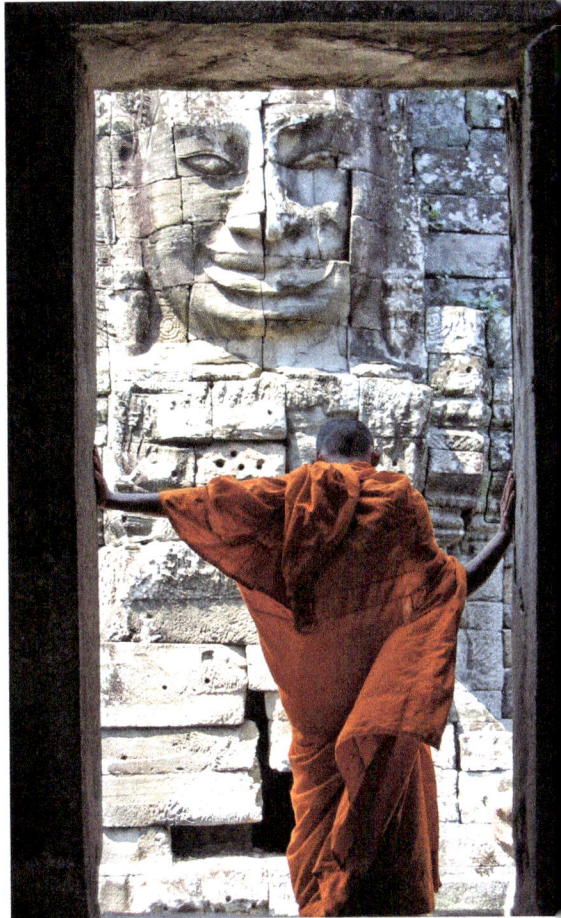

*Ancient face smiles down
upon a monk at Bayon.*

*Understanding
Cambodia today requires
comprehension of the
profound devastation
experienced by this
country during the era of
the "Killing Fields."*

Fruit vendor in the floating villages of Tonle Sap Lake.

One of the smallest of the temple sites, yet one of the most elaborately decorated of all. An enchanting, intricately carved, rose-colored temple at Banteay Srey.

Hotels can be socially responsible and luxurious, too.

Magnificent convergence of nature and man, as giant kapok trees weave themselves into the jungle temple of Ta Prohm.

Paul Dubrule Hotel and Tourism School for underprivileged young Cambodians.

Traditional dance performance given by students who were formerly street children.

Introduction to Responsible Travel *by Shoshana Kerewsky*

Nobody sets out on a trip with the goal of being an irresponsible tourist. Yes, some people just want to have fun without thinking about the consequences. Still, it is pretty much unheard of to plan a vacation with the intention of harming the people and the country you are about to visit.

Quite the opposite is true - most of us think of ourselves as responsible and ethical tourists, concerned about the wellbeing of the people we meet. In fact, an increasing number of people travel with the hope that their actions, money and conversations with people will be helpful. This introduction to socially responsible travel will help you know what to do, how to act and where your dollars will be best spent on your trip to Cambodia.

Simply put, "responsible travel," "socially responsible tourism," "ethical vacations," "intentional travel," and similar terms mean noticing and decreasing the negative effects of your visit while increasing the positive ones. Cambodia Tourism puts it this way: "Travelers take responsibility for their actions and behavior to ensure that their visit to an area is mutually beneficial both for travelers and local people."

Responsible travel considers social and cultural responsibility, environmental protection and economic sustainability. These values, known as the "triple bottom line" or "people, planet, profit" are recognized by the United Nations and have been ratified as a standard of accountability. In turn, you can be accountable for your own choices and actions. Whether the focus of your trip is sightseeing or volunteering, attention to these principles makes your trip more meaningful for you and for the communities you visit.

How each traveler takes responsibility will depend on a great variety of factors, but there are many ways to show respect and make sure that your trip benefits the communities you visit. These include some straight forward considerations, such as where to stay, where to eat, how to get around, the educational programs and entertainment to attend, where to shop and local travel arrangements. They also include more complex choices about how you act and interact.

Responsible Spending

It's nice to know that you can do the right thing just by spending your money intentionally. A dollar goes a long way in Cambodia and your choice of a socially responsible meal or necklace purchase may do more good than you would think.

Accommodations

You need to sleep somewhere, so why not stay where your payment makes the best economic and social impact? Some hotels are owned by big corporations or entrepreneurs from more affluent countries. Money spent at those hotels may leave Cambodia.

Locally-owned hotels are more likely to provide an economic benefit to local people and communities. Also, some are non-governmental organizations (NGOs). An NGO is a local organization that is not affiliated with the government. These are often not-for-profit and focused on humanitarian causes and projects. You'll also find hotels run by NGO affiliates and other programs that train or employ local people who are underprivileged, at risk or have been exploited in the past. Spending your money at these hotels provides local people with on-the-job education and a chance for a better life.

Unfortunately, sex tourism is still prevalent in Cambodia. One way you can help combat the sexual exploitation of women and children is to patronize hotels that work actively against the sex trade. You will learn more about this later in the book.

You will also want to consider the hotel's environmental and ecological practices. Some hotels have a reduce-reuse-recycle policy that will look familiar to many Americans but is a new idea in Cambodia. Since there is not a national plan or infrastructure to support green hotel management, this requires a big commitment and a lot of creativity on the part of the hotel.

For a real up-close and personal experience that benefits a family directly, you might even consider a home stay instead of a hotel. There's no better way to meet a Cambodian family and learn about their home life and culture.

Dining

Travelers are accustomed to thinking about *what* they eat, but don't always think about *why* they eat where they do. Restaurant decisions are often based on cost, perceived cleanliness and convenience. While these are reasonable considerations, it is also useful to gather more information about the restaurant's social practices. In the same way that some hotels provide training and employment for disadvantaged groups, some restaurants are also NGOs or hire the graduates of NGO restaurant training programs. Some are located in socially responsible hotels while others are independent.

You will have your choice of many clean, inexpensive restaurants, so narrow it down by looking for information describing the restaurant's relationship with an NGO, other training program, or local ownership. Choosing these restaurants sends a message that these practices make a difference.

Transportation

There is no shortage of transportation options in Cambodia. Taxis, cyclos (bicycle taxis), motorbike taxis and tuk-tuks (motorized rickshaws) will offer you a ride even if you'd rather walk! If you decide to hire one, look for the ChildSafe logo. You'll find it on the driver's hat, shirt, or helmet. This logo signifies that the driver has passed a training course in child protection. You can learn more about the ChildSafe Movement, which also works with hotels and other businesses, at www.childsafe-international.org/index.asp.

Educational and Cultural Programs

You can be a responsible tourist and at the same time learn about Cambodian culture, history and arts. Look for programs offered by non-profit organizations and museums. You will also find events that benefit non-profits, NGOs and other training programs, schools and medical services. These might include educational talks, musical performances, or traditional Cambodian dance.

It is possible to visit NGOs to see their programs in action, as well as find tours that visit local schools, rural communities and markets. Ecological and environmental tours are also available. Notice who is sponsoring the activity and where the profits will go.

More interactive programs give you an opportunity to talk with local people who are familiar with tourists and may have a good idea of what you don't know about their country or community. Do not hesitate to have conversations with people who can serve as cultural "translators."

Travel

You may want to be an ethical traveler but have a hard time putting together a complete vacation experience because you are not familiar with local businesses. Let one of Cambodia's socially responsible tour companies do the planning (see list in the back of this book). Look for tour operators associated with non-profit organizations or NGOs.

Ecotourism

The idea of environmentally-focused tourism is relatively new, though some travelers have always enjoyed visiting unique landscapes and habitats. According to the International Ecotourism Society, the term *ecotourism* refers to "responsible travel to natural areas that conserves the environment and improves the well-being of local people." Ecotourism in Cambodia provides an alternative way to make a living, one that preserves the environment. Instead of cutting down forests or poaching endangered wildlife, some Cambodians now work to save Cambodia's ecosystems. Some learn to lead bird-watching and nature tours, while others who live near national parks offer meals, oxcart rides, guided nature hikes and boat trips.

Shopping

On some Cambodian streets, it is hard to find a shop where your purchase does not benefit someone local or in need. Many NGOs run gift shops serve as training programs, or sell products that are made in training workshops, or both. In some, you can see artisans at work dyeing silk or weaving baskets. In others, product tags might inform you that the spices are grown and harvested in a rural community that practices sustainable agriculture or participates in fair trade, or that the handicraft is made by people who have been injured by land mines. Take advantage of Cambodia's distinctive offerings to choose gifts that are not only unique, but also socially responsible.

Acting and Interacting

Being Respectful

Again, it is the rare traveler who goes to another culture with the intention of being disrespectful. However, sometimes we are disrespectful without intending to be. This often happens because travelers assume that local customs are similar to their own, or just don't think about what respectful behaviors might be before leaving home.

Some of the ways that you can show respect and not give offense are common sense, yet tourists sometimes seem to leave their common sense at home. One of the most glaring examples is skimpy dress. Modest dress is the Cambodian standard, so men and women should wear shirts that cover their shoulders and pants or skirts at least to the knee. Longer pants or skirts may be required for religious sites. In an area with lots of tourists this dress code may not be obvious at first, but away from urban centers you risk giving offense (and being bitten by mosquitoes) if you are not appropriately covered.

Do not assume that Cambodians speak English. While many do, there are also many who don't. In tourist areas, where English is more common, hamburgers and pizza are the foods of choice and prices are marked in dollars, it can be easy to forget that some people won't understand you. Learn enough Khmer (Cambodian language) to thank people who help you.

Some ways of showing respect must be learned. Notice when other people take off their shoes. Shoes typically are not worn into houses and are not worn in Buddhist temples. There may be other establishments where shoes are also removed outside. If you are uncomfortable going completely barefoot, carry a pair of socks with you and change into them before entering shoe-free areas.

Since strong emotional expression is frowned upon, getting angry and raising your voice is not going to get you what you want. Instead, it may embarrass the Cambodians around you. Try responding to adversity the Cambodian way, by laughing and shrugging it off.

You probably know that you should ask permission before taking photos of people. You might not know that images of the Buddha should not be used as a background for photos of you or your friends, or that the soles of your feet should not be pointed toward images of the Buddha or other people, or that patting someone on the head is offensive. You may want to get a closer look at an architectural detail, just remember that that structure is somebody's home.

To avoid embarrassment or giving offense, a guidebook that includes local etiquette can be very helpful. *Cambodia: The Essential Guide to Customs and Culture* from Culture Smart! is a good place to begin. Remember that you won't offend anyone or get in trouble by being too polite or too respectful!

Giving Money Directly

The poverty in Cambodia can be a shock for some travelers. Tourists may be approached by begging children, especially at sites such as the Angkor Wat, markets and restaurants. The children may speak to you in English, tell you they love you and present an appealing and heartbreaking picture.

The solution may seem to be to give money directly to the children, but organizations like ChildSafe strongly recommend against this for a number of reasons. Perhaps the most compelling one is that begging keeps children on the street, where they are vulnerable to exploitation and harm. Some street children are being exploited, abused, or trafficked. Instead, support organizations that provide services for vulnerable children and youths. If it is hard for you to refuse begging, practice assertively saying "no thank you" before you go.

Giving directly to a local organization may also be risky. For example, an orphanage may be a front for corrupt people to pocket donations from tourists. To be sure that your money is actually helping people in need, always check out organizations before making a donation.

There are some circumstances where giving money to people directly may be appropriate, such as tipping. The average Cambodian income is about $1 a day, so your tip is welcome. At religious sites you may see people making donations or contributions and receiving sticks of incense to place on an altar. If you see Cambodians giving someone money, a small donation may be appropriate if you would like to make one. You may want to tip musicians or other performers. Use your best judgment and if you are not sure, don't give money.

The Environment

Obviously, don't litter. Perhaps not so obviously, be aware of the huge amount of plastic waste that is generated just by drinking bottled water. Rather than contributing several empty water bottles to the trash every day, consider getting some of your very necessary hydration by drinking water has been heated to a boil (like tea) or at restaurants that provide purified water. Alternatively, buy larger bottles of water to refill your water bottle that you have brought from home. To purify your own water, you can add .5 cc of a 2% tincture of iodine to a quart of water, let sit for half an hour and then add 1/8 teaspoon of vitamin C or Emergen-C to get rid of the iodine taste. To the extent that you can reuse plastic bags (or not use them at all), you help keep Cambodia clean.

Keeping Cambodia in Your Heart

Many people who care about responsible travel are moved by the spirit of the Cambodian people. Your trip may end, but your desire to help may well continue. You can make a significant difference in the lives of Cambodians by donating to a non-profit organization that assists those whose needs are greatest. Friendship with Cambodia helps landmine survivors, families living with HIV/AIDS, street children, trafficked girls and the rural poor. Our programs empower people to help themselves, primarily through micro-credit programs and education. We want to create long-term solutions.

How to Become a ChildSafe Traveler

Visitors to Cambodia, with the best of intentions, engage in behaviors that sustain or even further increase the risk of marginalized children. Giving money to begging children or buying products from them does little to address the serious problems these children face: lack of education, health care, or a supportive family environment. In fact, giving money to street children often leads to a lifestyle that ends in drugs, prostitution and crime.

Most tourists are unaware that corruption in orphanages is extremely common. Some institutions purport to protect children, but exploit them for their own gain. They often encourage parents to give up their children so they can create the appearance of greater need to garner contributions from unsuspecting tourists that donate their time, money or both.

The ChildSafe Movement encourages travelers to play an important role in safeguarding children. Learn to look at the situation differently and actively participate in helping children move away from life on the streets.

Tips for Travelers

Avoid buying from children and refrain from giving to begging children.
Directly helping them keeps them on the streets and places them at risk. If you really want to help, support organizations providing services that help these children and their families have a better future.

Purchase products made by parents or youth-in-training.
When you buy products made by parents or youth-in-training it gives them a regular income and a better future.

Avoid situations and actions that may lead to child exploitation.

Be aware that certain "tourist-attractions" such as orphanage or slum tours exploit children's vulnerabilities for financial gain. An orphanage is a child's home, a place that should be safe and should respect his/her right to privacy and dignity.

Taking children back to your hotel room for any reason is not a good idea.

You might be suspected as a pedophile when taking children to your hotel room. The penalties for child sex offenders are severe.

Avoid places that tolerate prostitution.

A high percentage of sex workers are minors. By supporting businesses that tolerate prostitution you are supporting an environment that places children at risk. Do not hesitate to report cases.

Keep your eyes wide open.

If you see a child in danger call the **ChildSafe Hotline 012-311-112** and report it. The hotline is open 24 hours/7 days a week. Whenever possible, we ask the caller to stay near the child until our team arrives to take appropriate action to protect the child.

ChildSafe
MOVEMENT
TOGETHER, PROTECTING CHILDREN

Support ChildSafe Movement Members.

ChildSafe trains local hotel staff and taxi drivers to protect children from abusive situations. Look for the ChildSafe logo during your travels and use their services.

www.thinkchildsafe.org
Facebook @ChildSafeMovement

Directory of Services, Activities, & Volunteer Opportunities

Your interactions in Cambodia will be greatly enriched by making responsible choices regarding places to stay, where you eat, shop, visit, or volunteer. The following chapters on Phnom Penh, Siem Reap, Sihanoukville and Kampot give a brief description of each city, feature itinerary highlights and list responsible businesses that we recommend. We were very selective in our process and have visited most of these businesses.

Criteria used to evaluate responsible business practices:

1. The business/organization supports environmental, cultural, social and historical programs.

2. The business/organization treats its staff with respect and pays fair wages.

3. Policies against child-trafficking and sex tourism are enforced.

4. The business is Khmer or locally-owned with profits staying in Cambodia.

5. The business/organization's products and practices help sustain the local people, environment and economy.

Most of these businesses are run by NGOs, hire staff trained by an NGO program, or donate profits to NGO projects. An NGO is a non-governmental organization, similar to a non-profit. Many are focused on humanitarian and environmental causes and projects.

Accommodation price guide in US Dollars:

$	under $20
$$	$20 - $50
$$$	$50 - $100
$$$$	$100 and up

We did not include pricing for restaurants as they are all in the under $20 range. The average price at most restaurants is $7 and under.

At the time of printing, the information in the listings was accurate. Tourism in Cambodia is growing very quickly. On that note, we anticipate that some of the businesses may move, raise their prices, or change hours. For current updates, additions and corrections to these listings, see our website at www.friendshipwithcambodia.org.

You can also help us keep this book updated by sending your suggestions and corrections to info@friendshipwithcambodia.com.

Tip: Before you start out, ask your taxi driver to call the business for directions (we have listed local phone numbers for each business). It can save you time, assure that you reach your destination and that the business is open.

Phnom Penh

The capital city of Phnom Penh (pop: 1,501,725), with its French colonial charm, is located at the confluence of the Mekong, Tonle Sap and Tonle Bassac rivers. The bustling capital city can be challenging with its non-stop traffic jams, noise, pollution and crowds. It can also be enticing with the cultural treasures of the Royal Palace, the outstanding collection of ancient sculpture at the National Museum and its colorful festivals and sunset cruises. It has remembrances of the genocide at Toul Sleng Museum, a former Khmer Rouge prison and the Killing Fields Memorial. Intersperse these visits with a walk on the waterfront, a ride in a tuk-tuk and great shopping at NGO boutiques.

Itinerary Highlights

Day 1

- Visit the National Museum (ancient sculpture) and Reyum Museum (contemporary exhibits).

- Have lunch at Daughters of Cambodia Café, step into their Visitor Center to learn about their work to stop human trafficking. Shop at their boutique and get a pedicure at their spa.

- In the afternoon tour the Toul Sleng Genocide Museum and shop across the street at VillageWorks, Khmer Life, Phaly Craft and CHA.

- Have dinner at Friends the Restaurant, shop next door at Friends 'n' Stuff.

- In the evening watch a Khmer dance and shadow puppet performance at Sovanna Phum (Friday and Saturday).

Day 2

- Visit the Royal Palace in the morning, then take a city tour in a tuk-tuk and enjoy the riverfront and parks, ending up at the Russian Market.

- Have lunch at Café Yejj.

- After your meal, shop at nearby Rajana and Peace Handicrafts. Treat yourself to something sweet at Jars of Clay.

- Have a relaxing dinner at Romdeng Restaurant.

- In the evening get a massage by the blind at Seeing Hands or have a drink and hear live music (on the weekends) at Chinese House.

Day 3

- In the morning take a bike tour on Mekong Island (very few cars) and see silk weaving and rural life. Or visit the Killing Fields Memorial.

- Have lunch at Lotus Blanc. Shop nearby at Tabitha for a wide variety of gifts.

- Visit Wat Phnom, a popular city park with wild monkeys and a temple on top of a hill. Stop for a cup of coffee and a treat at Java Café. Finish your shopping on trendy Street 240 at AND Boutique, Lotus Silk, Mekong+, Elsewhere and The 240 Boutique.

- Go for dinner at at La Pergola and watch a film at Meta House.

See Detail Map

Mekong River

Tonle Sap River

Chroy Changvar Friendship Bridge

The Old Stadium

Boeng Kak Lake

0 200 400 600 800 1000 m

Train Station

Wat Phnom

The Old Market

Kandal Market

Sisowath Quay

Pochentong International Airport

Confederation de la Russie - Pochentong Rd.

Kampuchea Krom Blvd.

Tchecoslovaquie

Nehru Blvd.

Charles De Gaul Blvd.

Monivong Blvd.

Norodom Blvd.

National Museum

The Royal Palace

The Silver Pagoda

Preah Sihanouk Quay

Mao Tse Toung Blvd.

Charles De Gaul Blvd.

Monireth

The Olympic Stadium

Sihanouk Blvd.   Sihanouk Blvd.   Sihanouk Blvd.

Independence Monument

Mao Tse Toung Blvd.

C PSE Boutique and
Lotus Blanc Restaurant

Toul Sleng Genocide Museum

Monivong Blvd.

Norodom Blvd.

Sothearos Blvd.

Bassac River

Mao Tse Toung Blvd.

White Linen H

Russian Market

Monivong Blvd.

Norodom Blvd.

The Bak Lake

Monivong Bridge

Kbal Thnal Market

See Detail Map

Wat Klang Kleang (15 km)
Oudong (45 km)
Wat Prasat (17 km)

Ho Chi Minh City (230 km)
Tonle Bati (35 km)
Takeo (75 km)

Tonle Sap River

H Hotel	R Restaurant	A Arts & Culture
C Craft Shop	m Massage	T Transportation

R **Chinese House**

M

Wat Phnom

m **Seeing Hands 1**

Sisowath Quay

The Old Market

Kandal Market

Sisowath Quay

H **Quay**

The Central Market

Norodom Blvd.

m **Hands & Feet Spa**
C R **Daughters of Cambodia**
C **A.N.D. Boutique**
R **FCC Phnom Penh**
C **Craft Village**

C **Friends**
Frangipani Royal Palace H
Frangipani Fine Arts H C **Sentosa**
Ta Prohm R
Reyum A
Connecting Hands R
Romdeng The National Museum
Blue Lime H
C R **Friends**
La Pergola R
The Plantation H

Sothearos Blvd.

Sisowath Quay

The Royal Palace

The Silver Pagoda

Monivong Blvd.

Mekong+
Lotus Silk C C C
Elswhere C R C
The 240 C R
R **Bloom**
AAC Showroom C
C **A.N.D. Boutique**
Pavilion H

X **Kantha Bopha Children's Hospital**

C **Cambodian Creations**

A **Meta House**

M

H **Tea House**
H **Frangipani Villa-60s**

H **Kabiki**

Sihanouk Blvd

Lucky X
Market
Anise H
Smateria C
Pidan Khmer C

The Independence Monument

Sihanouk Blvd.

R **Java**
La Rose H

Kapko Market

m **Seeing Hands 2B**

Mad Monkey H

Lotus Blanc R

Nor

Seeing Hands 2B ⓜ

Mad Monkey 𝐻

Lotus Blanc 🄁

Smart Craft 🄲
Villageworks 🄲 🄲 Khmer Lifelong
Toul Sleng 🄲 CHA
Genocide
Museum

Tabitha 🄲

Phaly Craft 🄲

Watthan Artisans 🄲

Boeng Keng
Kang Market

Frangipani Villa-90s 𝐻
Rambutan 𝐻

Mao Tse Toung Blvd.

Monivong Blvd.

Norodom Blvd.

𝐻 Frangipani Living Arts

Russian
Market

Jars 🄁 🄁 Café Yejj
of Clay 🄲 🄲 Ta Prohm
Rajana
Peace Handicrafts

Tra Bek
Lake
(being
filled in for
development)

Kroma Clothes 🄲
🄰 Sovanna Phum

Where to Stay

Anise Hotel and Restaurant

#2 Street 278 off Street 57
Near Independence Monument
phone: 023 222 522
www.anisehotel.com.kh

$$ - $$$

Providing personalized accommodation and restaurant services to business and leisure travelers. All rooms include AC, mini-bar, TV and DVD player, in-room safe, hair dryer and internet connection. Anise is a ChildSafe member.

Blue Lime

#42 Street 19z
Street 19z is off Street 19, across from the Royal Institute of Fine Arts, at the back of the National Museum
phone: 023 222 260
www.bluelime.asia

$$ - $$$

A 14-room urban accommodation set in a lush exotic garden with a swimming pool. Centrally located between the National Museum and Royal Palace. The rooms, garden and pool are modern minimalist, with concrete furniture and free wireless internet. The bar/restaurant serves food in the garden lounge and you can enjoy cocktails in the pool. All guests should be over 16 years old. Blue Lime supports ChildSafe, has zero tolerance for sex tourism and uses innovative solar water heating.

FCC Hotel Phnom Penh

363 Sisowath Quay
Near the National Museum
phone: 023 210 142
www.fcccambodia.com

$$$ - $$$$

Renowned for its views, the hotel and restaurant overlooks the convergence of the Mekong and Tonle Sap rivers. The National Museum, Royal Palace and Silver Pagoda are all within walking distance and the capital's bustling riverfront entertainment district is just outside the doors. Offering 10 spacious boutique rooms, Foreign Correspondence Club (FCC) promotes environmentally friendly work practices, invests in responsible job opportunities, and supports many NGOs that are valuable contributors to the community.

Five Frangipani Socially Responsible Hotels

Many of the hotel staff are hired from Friends International and Pour un Sourire d'Enfant, training programs for underprivileged youth. All Frangipani hotels are "absolutely against sex tourism" and are committed to protecting youth and children from all forms of abuse.

Frangiapani Villa-60's

#20R Street 252
Between Monivong Boulevard and Street 63

Frangiapani Villa-90's

#25 Street 71
Near Monivong Boulevard and
Mao Tse Toung
phone: 012 687 717
www.frangipanihotel.com

$$ - $$$

Frangiapani Villa-60s and 90s boutique hotels offer beautifully-restored examples of modern Khmer architecture. Villa 60's has 7 rooms, a terrace café, is centrally located, and is a few minutes' walk from a good selection of restaurants. Villa 90's has 15 rooms, a garden café and is a short tuk-tuk ride from the Russian market and other popular sites. Both have wi-fi and include a complimentary breakfast.

Frangipani Living Arts Hotel & Spa

#15 Street 123
Near the Russian Market
phone: 023 223 320
www.frangipanilivingarts.com

$$$$

A 10-story hotel four star hotel with 123 guest rooms, most with balconies. Offers two swimming pools, a spa, and business center. The rooftop bar and lounge have a view of the city. The restaurant serves Asian and Western food.

Frangipani Fine Arts Hotel

#43 Street 178
Near the Royal Palace
phone: 016 581 045
www.frangipanifineart-hotel.com

$$$

Tucked away down a quiet side alley close to the campus of the School of Fine Arts, this contemporary boutique hotel has 22 guest rooms on three floors around a leafy courtyard. The attractive furnishings are in wood, silk and other natural materials manufactured by leading Cambodian producers. Their restaurant serves fine Royal Khmer and French cuisines and offers a large selection of wine and cocktails. Complimentary breakfast, wi-fi, and use of guest bicycles.

Kabiki

#22 Street 264
Off of Street 19, near Independence Monument
phone: 023 222 290
www.thekabiki.com

$$$

Beautiful family friendly accommodations. 11 rooms, all with bathrooms, hot water, AC, fridge, safety deposit box and cable TV. Other features include a 17m pool, kiddie pool, internet access, playground, bicycle and roller-skate tracks, special children's menu and free wireless internet. Kabiki is a ChildSafe member, has zero tolerance for sex tourism and uses innovative solar designs for water heating.

La Rose Suites

#4 Street 21
Off Sihanouk Boulevard
East of Independence Monument
phone: 023 222 254
www.larosesuites.com

$$$$

Five-star boutique hotel with 68 suites. Amenities include a salt-water pool, free minibar, wi-fi, a free one-hour traditional Khmer massage and a fitness center. The hotel hires graduates from NGO training programs for disadvantaged youth and provides assistance to families in need. Short-term volunteer opportunities for guests, such as teaching English at a local school, digging wells and painting houses.

Mad Monkey
Backpackers Hostel

#26 Street 302
Off Monivong Boulevard
phone: 023 987 091
www.madmonkeyhostels.com

$ - $$

Offers 150 beds in dorm, double, and family rooms. All rooms have AC and hot water. Strict no-drugs or sex tourism policies. Staff make above minimum wage, have maternity benefits and educational allowances. Mad Monkey funds and supports arts organizations promoting the talents of young Cambodians.

Quay Hotel Phnom Penh

#277 Sisowath Quay
Near the National Museum
reservations: 023 992 284
phone: 023 224 894
www.thequayhotel.com

$$$ - $$$$

This minimalist 16-room hideaway is urban and relaxed. The hotel is an easy stroll to the National Museum, the Royal Palace, the Silver Pagoda, inviting cafes, designer shops and art galleries. The Quay supports Cambodia Rugby, Family Care and ChildSafe. Phnom Penh's first carbon-friendly and environmentally sound hotel.

Rambutan Resort

#29 Street 71
Off Mao Tse Toung Boulevard
Near Sihanouk Boulevard
phone: 017 992 240
www.rambutanresort.com

$$$

Catering to travelers looking for privacy in the center of Phnom Penh, the gay-friendly Rambutan Resort consists of a city villa in Khmer style of the '60 and a newly- built modern wing overlooking a salt-water pool with waterfall, pool-bar and restaurant set in a lush tropical garden. Rates include breakfast. The hotel sponsors a scholarship program and partners with NGOs.

The Pavilion

#227 Street 19
Near Street 240 and the Royal Palace with a small guarded gate entrance
phone: 023 222 280
www.thepavilion.asia

$$ - $$$

A tranquil oasis a few steps from the Royal Palace, Wat Botum and the Royal Pagoda. This collection of four French-Khmer historic buildings sits amongst lush gardens. Amenities include two large swimming pools, two lounges serving food and drinks, a spa, gym and Cambomania shop. They are committed to responsible tourism, urban heritage conservation and cultural awareness.

The Plantation

#28 Street 184
Near the Royal Palace
phone: 023 21 51 51
www.theplantation.asia

$$$-$$$$An urban resort ideally located in the heart of Phnom Penh Historic District. A green oasis of lush gardens, ponds and pools. Features a spa, beauty salon and a gym. The poolside restaurant serves Western, Asian and Khmer cuisines including vegetarian meals and a salad bar. Cambomania boutique offers gifts, fashion, unique local products and objet d'art. Actively involved in the promotion of local art, environment-friendly initiatives and community activities.

Tea House

#32 Street 242
Near Street 51
phone: 023 212 789
www.maads.asia/teahouse

$$-$$$

Streamlined and stylish, rooms include free wi-fi, buffet breakfast, AC and mini-bar. Facilities include a swimming pool, restaurant, Tea Garden and spa. The Tea Lounge serves 30 varieties of tea, hot or iced, and signature tea cocktails. Boutique gift shop offers handicrafts, spices, jewelry and stylish clothing cut from all-natural fabrics. Promotes sustainable and responsible tourism.

White Linen Boutique Hotel

#227 Street 442
West of the Russian Market
phone: 023 997 120
www.daughtersofcambodia.org

$$

Five elegant custom-designed rooms in a light and airy layout. Rooms have A/C, satellite TV, DVD, wi-fi and a safe. Has an on-site restaurant. Run by Daughters of Cambodia NGO. Directly benefits Cambodian victims of human trafficking.

Restaurants

Bloom Creations Café

#40 Street 222
Off of Street 63
phone: 077 757 500
www.bloom-asia.org
10am to 5pm, closed Sunday

A chic oasis to unwind, this cake art gallery is run by a not-for-profit organization that empowers and skills underprivileged Cambodian women and trafficking survivors. Offers fair trade coffee, cupcakes and greeting cards.

Café Yejj

#170 Street 450
Near the Russian Market
phone: 092 600 750
Facebook @CafeYejj
8am to 9pm, daily

A bistro café in the popular Russian Market area. European décor, wireless internet, tantalizing pastas, crisp salads, wraps, chilled lassi, delicious brownie sundae and cheesecake. The café provides skills training and employment in catering and hospitality to women who are "at risk" and from vulnerable backgrounds.

Chinese House

#45 Sisowath Quay
Along the river, opposite the port
phone: 092 553 330
www.restaurant-phnompenh.com
11am to 1am Monday to Friday, 11am to 2am Saturday, 11am to midnight Sunday

A fusion restaurant, elegant lounge bar and art gallery. Live music on the weekends. Run by the owners of The Pavilion, leaders in responsible tourism and the use of environmentally sustainable practices.

Connecting Hands Café

#13 Street 178
Behind the National Museum
phone: 078 588 810
www.connectinghands.com.au
9am to 6pm, closed Sunday

Enjoy a breakfast burrito, veggie burger, chicken wrap, fresh ground coffee or a fresh fruit smoothie. A training restaurant for young women who were victims of sexual slavery. Run by an Australian NGO.

Daughters of Cambodia Café

#321 Sisowath Quay
Along the river
phone: 089 910 203
www.daughtersofcambodia.org
9am to 6pm, closed Sunday

Brunch or lunch overlooking the river. Start with a healthy salad and end with a chocolate brownie. Run by an NGO from New Zealand. Directly benefits victims of human trafficking.

Friends the Restaurant

#215 Street 13
Near National Museum,
cross street Street 178
phone: 012 802 072
www.friends-international.org
11am to 10pm, daily

A friendly and popular gathering place serving western and Asian tapas. A training restaurant run by former street youth and their teachers. All proceeds from the restaurant go to Friends-International projects for street children.

Jars of Clay

#39 Street 155
Near the Russian Market
phone: 012 800 160
www.jarsofclay.asia
7:30am to 9pm, closed Sunday

Unique range of Western home-style cooking, delicious cakes, teas, coffees and healthy juices. A social enterprise providing sustainable employment for at-risk young Cambodian women. Offers staff shareholding opportunity, pays good salaries and provides staff with access to education scholarships.

Java Café and Gallery

#56 Sihanouk Boulevard
Near the Independence Monument
7am to 10pm
phone: 012 833 512
www.javacambodia.org

A unique combination of a restaurant and non-profit gallery promoting the development of contemporary art in Cambodia. Enjoy delicious homemade food, desserts, great coffee, a refreshing drink or cocktail.

Eating at Friends Restaurant

I was wondering just what to expect at the restaurant staffed by former street kids. Is this going to be fun or work? The answer is... fun! Excellent food, prepared and served by young people happy to be learning the restaurant business, in a very cheerful environment. The whole experience is uplifting and positive.

The food is varied and tasty, getting votes from some in our group for best food in Cambodia. There are two enticing cookbooks for sale. On the walls, original art adds to the attractiveness of the space.

Friends Restaurant and the art on its walls are some of the successes of Mith Samlanh, an organization that works with former street children and youth to provide vocational training and employment. It is a joy to see this project doing well and to be well fed as a bonus.

Lowell Hill

La Pergola

#28 Street 184
At The Plantation Hotel
phone: 071 461 5168
Facebook @lapergola.phnompenh
6pm to 10pm

Colorful and refreshing modern French and Khmer cuisine. Beautiful ambience, a peaceful haven overlooking the hotel's elegant courtyard. Has the best Fish Amok, the signature dish of Cambodia. Supports local arts and responsible tourism.

Lotus Blanc (2 locations)

#152 Street 51
Near Street 310
phone: 017 602 251
www.pse.ngo
7am to 10pm Monday to Friday

A heart-centered dining experience with delicious French and Asian food. Run by Pour un Sourire d'Enfant (NGO) offering a vocational training program for youth who live in poverty near the garbage dump. Wireless Internet is available.

Second location:
Village Trea Stung Mean Chey
On the outskirts of town
Call for directions
phone: 012 598 002
7am to 9:30pm Monday to Friday,
7am to 2pm Saturday, closed Sunday

Choose from an à la carte or 3-course set menu of French and Asian cuisine served by smiling and eager students. They offer a fantastic buffet every Friday. Shop in their lovely boutique. You can schedule a tour of their school and vocational training center.

Romdeng Restaurant

#74 Street 174
Cross street Street 51, one block from Norodom
phone: 092 219 565
www.friends-international.org
11am to 10pm, daily

Serving authentic Cambodian cuisine with a modern twist and set in a beautifully decorated house and garden. Students at the restaurant are former street youth who are now studying hospitality. All proceeds from the restaurant go to Friends-International (NGO) projects for street children.

The 240

#83 Street 240
phone: 017 368 937
www.maads.asia/the240
8am to 8pm

Healthy food café and coffee shop with a peaceful ambience with good service. Well-prepared and delicious wraps, salads, smoothies, and fresh juices. Owners support responsible tourism.

Craft Shops

A.N.D. Boutique (2 locations)

First location: #52 Street 240
Second location: #3 Street 178
Near the river
phone: 023 224 713
Facebook @artisandesigners

Merging traditional Cambodian hand-skills with contemporary fashion. Hand-woven cotton ikat dresses, tops and pants. Handbags and jewelry. Supports producers living with disabilities.

Artisans' Association of Cambodia (AAC) Showroom

#11b, Street 240
Between Norodom Boulevard and Street 51
phone: 023 213 904
www.aac.org.kh

An NGO fair-trade association that supports over 40 handicraft groups across Cambodia. Some of the nation's most vulnerable people are benefited, including landmine victims, those living with HIV/AIDS, street children and minority tribes' people.

Cambodian Creations

A small lane off Street 240
Next to Artillery Café
phone: 097 522 3043
www.cambodiancreations.com
9am to 6pm, daily
Charming toys, jewelry, and silks from three established social enterprises Cambodia Knits, Khmer Creations, and Fairweave. Income generation for at-risk Cambodians.

Cambodia Handicraft Association for Land Mine and Polio Disabled (CHA)

#28 Street 330
In front of Toul Sleng Genocide Museum
phone: 012 916 796
7:30am to 5:30pm, daily
www.cha-cambodia.org

A Cambodian run NGO, that teaches handicraft skills to landmine and polio-disabled adults, enabling them to produce a range of beautiful silk products. CHA provides a home and a friendly working environment in which to learn. The association has enabled over 150 disabled to return to their communities with new skills and the possibility of a brighter future.

Craft Village

#375 Sisowath Quay
On the river near Foreign Correspondence Club
phone: 095 753 787
www.craftvillage.biz
Silk scarves hand-woven by women living in remote villages. Skilled artisans are paid

a fair price for their intricate work and are given a sustainable income to keep their traditions alive. Eco-friendly and AZO free.

Daughters of Cambodia Boutique & Visitors Center

#321 Sisowath Quay
Along the river
phone: 089 910 203
www.daughtersofcambodia.org
9am to 6pm, closed Sunday

Lovely fashion accessories, jewelry, and home furnishings. The Visitor Center has an exhibit and film about helping those trapped in sex-exploitation and trafficking. This New Zealand NGO helps them recover through counseling, training, employment, and learning how to sustain their new life-style in non-institutional settings.

Elsewhere Shop

#54 Street 240
phone: 012 414 596
www.elsewhere2.asia

Local fashion at its best. Clothes & accessories. Cambodian-made designs from natural fabrics. Owners support responsible tourism.

Friends 'n' Stuff (2 locations)

First location: #215 Street 13 Off of Street 178
Next to Friends the Restaurant
11am to 9pm, daily
Second location: #74 Street 174
At Romdeng Restaurant
Off of Norodom Boulevard
11am to 10:30pm, daily
phone: 092 219 565
www.friendsnstuff.org

A colorful shop offering a wide range of products designed by Mith Samlanh/Friends-

International (NGO) students in training and by parents of former street children. Choose from hand-crafted purses, clothing, necklaces, hand bags and recycled products as well as a selection of second-hand goods. The Nail Bar, located in Friends 'n' Stuff, is run by students from Mith Samlanh's beauty class.

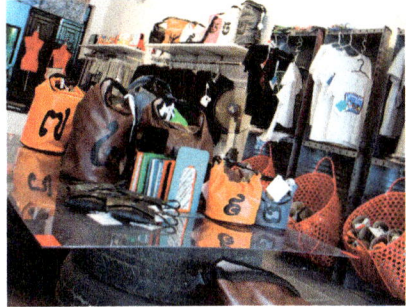

Khmer Life

#118a Street 330
Opposite Toul Sleng Museum entrance
phone: 012 592 098
Facebook @KhmerLife

An NGO shop providing job opportunities to students from poor families to help rebuild hope and dignity in their communities. Natural materials are used to produce unique designs on cushion covers, tea towels, curtains and other useful products.

Kroma Clothes Shop

South on Monivong Boulevard
At Boeung Trabek High School
phone: 023 694 4449
kroma.clothes.shop@online.com.kh

Large selection of Khmer silks, cotton clothing, bags, housewares and toys made at the Cambodia Japan Friendship Training Center.

Lotus Silk

#57 Street 240
phone: 023 210 215
www.lotus-silk.com

Ethical fashion and hand-crafted accessories that preserve traditional skills and provide fair income to disadvantaged women. Unique products that are environmentally sustainable, using organically grown silk and upcycled fabrics.

Mekong Plus

#49 Street 240
phone: 023 219 607
www.mekong-plus.com

Hand crafted quilts and accessories. A social enterprise creating sustainable employment for under-privileged rural women.

Peace Handicrafts and Silks

#39 Street 155
By the SE corner of the Russian Market
phone: 023 993 331
www.peacehandicraft.com
7:30am to 5pm, Monday to Saturday

High quality hand-woven silk products carefully handcrafted by highly skilled artisans using traditional processes. Providing training and employment opportunities for landmine victims, polio-disabled persons and the underprivileged. Many trainees have become self-supporting, confident artisans.

Phaly Craft

#37 Street 113
Off of Street 360
Near Toul Sleng Museum
phone: 092 94 59 54
www.phalycraft.com

Silk handbags, ties, and ornaments made by disadvantaged women and the disabled. Profits support Future Light Orphanage and preserve traditional weaving.

Pidan Khmer

#170 Street 63
South of Sihanouk Boulevard
phone: 023 210 849
www.cyk.org.kh

Traditional ikat weave and natural dyes make their products very special. Made from hand-loomed silk and cotton from Takeo and Kandal Provinces. Run by the Japanese NGO Caring for Young Khmer.

PSE Boutique

Village Trea Stueng Mean Chey
On the outskirts of town
Have your driver call for directions
phone: 012 598 002
www.pse.ong/en/visit-cambodia
8am to 5pm, Monday to Friday and 8am to noon, Saturday

Pour un Sourire d'Enfant NGO has a sewing

training and employment for the mothers of families experiencing great difficulty, enabling them to rebound in life. Creating hats, scarves, bags, clothing, and interior decoration. Located next to their excellent French restaurant.

Rajana (2 locations)

First location: #170 Street 450
Near the Russian Market
Second location: #55 Street 240
8am to 6pm, daily
phone: 023 993 642
www.rajanacrafts.org

NGO made, fair trade products are created by combining traditional Cambodian skills with contemporary designs. Young rural and urban poor Cambodians are trained in the production and marketing of handicrafts, helping them provide an income for themselves and their families.

Sentosa Silk

#33 Sothearos Boulevard
Corner of Street 178, Near the
National Museum
phone: 023 222 974
Facebook @Sentosa Silk
8am to 7pm, daily

A social enterprise promoting Khmer silk and supporting disabled Cambodians and poor youth who have no regular source of income. Sentosa offers beautiful silk products that are made by disabled women who have been NGO trained.

Smart Craft

#82 Sothearos Street
Near Toul Sleng Museum
phone: 012 633 938
Facebook @SmartCraft

Rajana

Rajana's selection of crafts, jewelry and locally grown spices is fantastic. I've decorated my office with their silk wall hangings. The colors are luminous and bright, filling my work area with lotuses and vines in hot pink, pumpkin orange and lime green. I also have a necklace and earrings crafted from scavenged brass from old bomb casings - a moving example of beating swords into plowshares. The earrings are inscribed with the Khmer word for "peace." I've brought my sister and friends silver jewelry from Rajana as well.

Shoshana Kerewsky

Made by Cambodian artisans with disabilities, improving their living standards. Offering a wide variety of products including wallets made from inner tubes, jewelry, silk and cotton scarves with natural dyes.

Tabitha

#239 Street 51, corner of Street 360
phone: 023 721 038
www.tabitha-cambodia.org
7am to 6pm, closed Sunday

An attractive craft shop with a large selection of hand-crafted items. Tabitha is a Christian organization whose purpose is to help the poor in Cambodia. Community development is the focus, with an emphasis on generating income and increasing savings, all of which will enable them to change those parts of their lives that keep them poor.

Smateria

#8 Street 57
South of Sihanouk Boulevard
Additional shops in the airports
phone: 023 211 701
www.smateria.com

Hip recycled bags and accessories that surprise you with their ingenuity. An Italian social enterprise that treats their employees well: 13-month salary, health insurance, training opportunities and free child care.

Ta Prohm Silks

#49 Street 178
Across from the National Museum
phone: 012 982 976
sam.taprohmsilk@gmail.com

Tastefully designed bags, scarves, pillows, and clothes from handwoven Cambodian silk. Chim Kong, the owner and designer, was twelve when she was injured by a landmine. Now she employs disabled people to make their products.

The 240 Boutique

#83 Street 240
phone: 017 368 937
Facebook @The 240
8am to 8pm

Lifestyles concept store with original art and unique gifts, next to their restaurant. Owners are committed to responsible tourism.

Villageworks Songkhem Collection

#118 Street 113/330
Across from Toul Sleng Museum
phone: 023 215 732
www.villageworks.biz
8am to 5pm, closed Sunday

Original handcrafted gifts made by people in small villages. Your support helps the villagers break free from their poverty cycle and find 'Songkhem' (hope) in life.

Watthan Artisans Cambodia

Wat Than Pagoda,
#180 Norodom Boulevard
phone: 023 216 321
www.wac.khmerproducts.com

A worker-run cooperative that helps Cambodians with landmine and polio disabilities to become artisans in handicrafts and woodcarving. The artisans receive fair wages and benefits, with profits shared by the staff and producers as well as being reinvested into staff development and training. All products are designed and produced on site at their workshop in Phnom Penh.

Arts & Culture

Meta House

#6 Street 264
South of Wat Botum and Independence
Monument, between Street 19 and
Suramarit Boulevard
phone: 023 224 140
www.meta-house.com
6pm to 12 midnight, Tuesday - Sunday
Gallery and screenings are free

Cambodia's first art/media/communication
center is defined as an interactive environment, offering an ongoing forum for
international/national artists. Exhibitions
and workshops are on the ground floor.
Intermediate floors display student works,
installations and a private collection of
paintings addressing themes of western,
Asian and Cambodian origin. The open-air
rooftop and bar screens feature films, video
art and documentaries.

Reyum Institute

#47 Street 178
Across from the National Museum
phone: 023 217 149

Dedicated to art, culture and education
in Cambodia. The activities of Reyum
include research, training and the sharing
of knowledge through exhibitions, seminars
and publications that aim to preserve and
promote arts and culture. Khmer books for
children are available at their store.

Sovanna Phum Art Association

#166 Street 99
Go south on Monivong Boulevard
Right on Street 484
phone: 010 337 552
Facebook @Sovannaphumtheatre
Performance at 7:30pm, Friday and Saturday
Adults 5 USD, Children 3 USD

An independent Khmer art association.
Sovanna Phum's focus is to preserve
the treasures of Khmer culture through
shadow puppet theatre, classical dance,
folk dance, traditional music, theatre and
circus. They also promote inter-cultural
exchange by interacting with artists from
other countries and by working with NGOs
and international organizations on different
educational awareness campaign projects.

Massage & Services

Hands & Feet Spa for Women

#321 Sisowath Quay
Along the river
phone: 089 910 203
www.daughtersofcambodia.org
9am to 6pm, closed Sunday
Luxuriate while supporting Daughters of
Cambodia, an NGO working to help free
women trapped in the Cambodian sex industry.

Massage Clinic by the Blind

#10 Street 118
phone: 012 269 141

Seeing Hands 1

#12 Street 13
In front of the Post Office near Wat Phnom
phone: 016 856 188

Seeing Hands 2A

#209 Street 63
Between Streets 310 and 322
Phone: 016 722 345
8am to 9pm daily
6 USD

Seeing Hands massage center by the blind,
featuring Japanese-style Anma and shiatsu
to release stress and tension.

Friends Nailbar

#215 Street 13
phone: 023 426748
www.mithsamlanh.org
Located in Friends 'n' Stuff Shop, next
to Friends the Restaurant and near the
National Museum.
11am to 9pm, daily

Offering manicures and pedicures given by the
students in beauty training at Mith Samlanh
(NGO). Indulge yourself! All profits are
shared between the students and the training
center and students gain first-hand experience
of the beauty industry.

Nigah, my Blind Masseuse

*Ahhhhhh.... I treated myself
to a massage at Seeing Hands
Massage, a business owned and
run by the blind. Nigah's touch
was soothing and professional, her
child-like voice full of enthusiasm
and curiosity. I liked her so much
and wanted to know more about
her life, so I asked her for tea the
next week. I thought it would be a
lovely experience for us but it was
more challenging than I imagined. I
learned how to guide her in and out
of the tuk-tuk, through crowded
broken down streets and narrow
aisle ways. I had great admiration
for her.*

*She told me that she became
blind at age one from a measles
infection. In 1993, she was accepted
into a program with Maryknoll to
learn Braille, literacy, orientation
and mobility. She then entered a
massage training program from
which she successfully graduated
and received a scholarship to
study massage in Japan. She
now continues to teach new
students and is a co-owner in this
self-supportive massage center.
We discussed the challenges of
a co-operative venture and her
handicap. She was open to helpful
suggestions and as I left, I booked
another massage with her.*

Pujita Mayeda

Siem Reap

Siem Reap is an energetic town (pop: 230,714) with lush Royal Gardens and a small river flowing through its center. Recently built up with hotels, there still are remnants of jungle with wild monkeys just outside of town. Siem Reap has an abundance of appealing restaurants and lodging to accommodate any budget.

It is from here that one goes to the temples of Angkor built by the Khmer civilization between 802 and 1432 AD. Each of the complexes have distinctive features; hundreds of huge carved faces at Bayon, the god and demon lined causeway of Angkor Thom, rose-colored intricate carvings at Banteay Srey and the five spiraling towers of renowned Angkor Wat, one of mankind's most remarkable architectural achievements. Angkor Wat is said to be the largest religious structure in the world, with its walls covered inside and out with bas-reliefs and carvings depicting Hindu epics and Khmer life. Although its name is often used for the entire site, Angkor Wat is just one of the structures in an enormous complex of hundreds of temples, terraces, lakes and monuments that spread across over three hundred square kilometers.

Unlike most of the temples of Angkor, Ta Prohm has been left in the condition in which it was found. Ruins precariously interlaced by the jungle's creeping kapok trees, have made this dramatic and photogenic temple one of the most visited sites and an ideal atmosphere for films such as Raiders of the Lost Ark. The vast number of temples in the area continues to grow as excavation continues to unearth the story of the Khmer civilization.

Visiting the temples in the early morning and the late afternoon allows the sun's shadows to bring out the intricate stone carvings and cast evocative hues on temple walls. Riding an elephant through the gate of Angkor Thom, shown on the cover of this book, is an option in the morning. Avoid the temples during the mid-day hours of oppressive heat

to Angkor Wat

Templation H
Bloom Garden H
Tonle Sap Exhibition A
Krousar Thmey Massage m
Landmine Museum A
Marum R

Peace Cafe R
Jaya House H
Friends 'n' Stuff C
AKA Fair Trade C

Blanc D'Angkor H
Earthwalkers
Paul Dubrule H R

Heritage
Suites H
Borann H

Charles De Gaulle

River Road

Rosy H
Chili Pepper R

Bou Savy H

Jasmine H

National Road No 6

National Road No 6

Sivatha Blvd.

Taphul Rd

Sivatha Blvd.

Oum Chhay Street

Street 2

Street 3

FCC

Pokambor Ave.

Siem Reap River

Babel H

Achar Sva St

Street 14

Frangipani H
Garden
Shinta Mani H R Kroya R

Oum Khum Street

Wat Bo Road

KKO X
Bike Tour

Frangipani H
Villa I & II

Street 5

Mad Monkey H

Angkor Hospital
for Childran X

Preah Sangreach Tep Vong St

Wat Bo
X

Common Grounds R

Auberge H
Mont Royal

The Villa H
Siem Reap

Pure! Bike Tour X
Central
Market R Hap Guan St
Blossom R

Bopha Angkor H

Soria Moria H R

Buttterflies Garden R C

Seeing Hands m

Three Seasons
C

New Leaf R

Pub Street

Susu C

Le Tigre A
Sao Mao
Old
Market

Sister Srey R

Mekong-Plus C

The Steakhouse R

Joe to Go R

7 Makara Rd

Night
Market

Haven R

ConCERT X

Phare Circus A

Angkor Night Market St

Artisans C
d' Angkor

Phka
Kravan
m

Sok San Rd

BBU Rd

Institute of Khmer Textiles
C

Sala Bai H R

0   200   400   600   800   1000 m

H Hotel   R Restaurant   A Arts & Culture
C Craft Shop   m Massage   T Transportation

and crowds. Thousands of people visit Angkor Wat and the other temples each day. A 3-day temple pass is 63 USD.

Spend at least three days in Siem Reap to have time to visit not only the temples, but also Tonle Sap Lake. This unique site is noted for its being the primary source of fish for Cambodia and for its annual rhythm of dramatic rising and falling water level, which is dependent upon the seasonal reversals of the Tonle Sap River.

Itinerary Highlights

Day 1

- View the extensive and fascinating bas reliefs at the Banyon Temple in the Angkor Wat complex. Afterward, visit Angkor Hospital for Children.
- Have lunch at Sala Bai Restaurant.
- Take a break after lunch and relax poolside or take a catnap in your room.
- In the late afternoon, visit Angkor Wat Temple and enjoy the sunset around 6 pm.
- Have a lovely dinner at Marun Restaurant and buy gifts at Friends 'N' Stuff crafts.

Day 2

- Take a morning boat ride and birdwatching trip with Sam Veasna Center or Osmose on Tonle Sap Lake and see floating villages and the local wildlife. Visit the Gecko Environmental Center and make a donation to protect this fragile resource.
- Have lunch at Kroya in Shinta Mani Hotel.
- In the afternoon visit Ta Prohm's picturesque temples covered in jungle. On the way back, stop at the Tonle Sap Exhibition.

- Dinner at Chili Pepper to watch a traditional dance and shadow puppet performance by Krousar Thmey's orphanage dance troupe on Wednesday.

Day 3

- Tour Banteay Srey Temple at sunrise, as the soft morning light bathes the intricate carvings at this incredibly beautiful site. It is a 40-minute drive from Siem Reap.
- On the way back to town, stop at The Cambodia Landmine Museum (near Banteay Srey).
- Have lunch at Le Jardin des Delices (Paul Dubrule Hotel and Tourism School).
- In the afternoon, visit the Artisans d'Angkor Silk Farm and Artisans d'Angkor craft center and workshop, continue shopping at Sao Mao and Susu near the Old Market. Visit Wat Bo Temple, where young monks like to practice their English with foreigners.
- Attend a yoga class and stay for dinner at Peace Café.
- In the evening, get a massage by the blind at Krousar Thmey or Seeing Hands.

Where to stay

Auberge Mont Royal

497 Taphul Road
phone: 012 630 131
www.auberge-mont-royal.com
$$ - $$$

A charming French-Khmer style boutique hotel set in a tranquil setting. Attractively furnished rooms have AC and a fridge. Facilities include a restaurant, spa, pool and internet. Between temple visits, you can get a manicure while relaxing at the pool. Auberge Mont Royal trains underprivileged youth in hotel skills and management.

Babel Guest House

#738 Wat Bo Road
phone: 078 858 469
www.babelsiemreap.com
$ - $$

Norwegian-owned guesthouse, with a tropical garden, outdoor restaurant and bar and a strong focus on responsible tourism. All the rooms have AC, cable TV, wi-fi and private bathrooms with hot showers. Babel runs an educational program that allows its staff and tuk-tuk drivers to work on their Bachelor degrees. Babel is a member of ChildSafe and ConCERT Cambodia.

Bloom Garden Guesthouse

Off Road 60
Drive beyond Ankor Wat Temple Ticket Booth, take second left (before Khmer Restaurant 333), Bloom is located 250 meters on the right.
phone: 063 969 291
www.bloomguesthouse.com
$$

A colonial villa in a tropical garden started by a Dutch NGO as a training program and social enterprise. Spacious rooms have A/C, hot showers and a mini-fridge. Tucked away from the crowds and traffic, you can enjoy the sound of birds singing.

Borann L'Auberge des Temples

Wat Bo Road
Near Royal Pavillion
phone: 063 964 740
www.borann.com
$$

Offering five inviting bungalows nestled in an exotic garden. Each room includes bathroom and individual terrace, but no TV or fridge. There is a swimming pool and private restaurant on-site. Borann partners with local humanitarian organizations and is a ChildSafe member.

Earthwalkers

Off of National Road #6
Toward the airport
phone: 012 967 901
www.angkorhotels.org/earthwalkers
$ - $$

A guesthouse providing affordable and comfortable rooms, a cozy bar, pool and restaurant. Free pick-up from airport, bus station or ferry terminal. Friendly and welcoming staff offer travel advice and will arrange transport and tour bookings for groups and individual travellers. Volunteer information available in lobby. Earthwakers is a ChildSafe member and supports many local charitable organizations.

FCC Hotel Angkor

Pokambor Avenue,
next to the Royal Residence
phone: 063 760 280
www.fcccambodia.com/fcc-hotel-angkor
$$$$

The old French Governor's mansion is now Foreign Correspondence Club (FCC) Angkor, a chic 31-room hotel of refined luxury and casual elegance. The hotel offers lush green gardens, a salt-water swimming pool, restaurant, bar and spa. Rooms are furnished in Cambodian textiles and named after local herbs and spices. FCC supports Cambodia Rugby, Family Care Cambodia and is a ChildSafe member.

Three Frangipani Socially Responsible Hotels

Many of the hotel staff are hired from training programs for underprivileged youth. All Frangipani hotels are "absolutely against sex tourism" and are committed to protecting children from all forms of abuse.

Frangipani Green Garden Hotel & Spa

#51 Oum Khun Street
phone: 063 963 342
www.greengardenhome.com
$$$

Sixteen guest rooms with Cambodian style furnishings set in a large garden compound in the heart of Siem Reap. Amenities include a pool, spa, restaurant, free wi-fi, A/C, mini-bar and fridge, and complementary airport transfer.

Frangipani Villa Hotels I & II

#603 Wat Bo Road
phone: 016 581 045
www.frangipanihotel.com
$$$

Adjacent to each other, each hotel has a pool and garden restaurant. There are a total of 87 spacious guest rooms. Included are wi-fi, complimentary breakfast, and the use of guest bicycles – great for exploring Siem Reap in the early morning.

Heritage Suites Hotel

Near Wat Polanka
phone: 063 969 100
www.heritagesuiteshotel.com
$$$$

Six rooms and 20 air-conditioned suites set in a lush garden with a pool. Bungalow suites include private steam rooms. Complimentary breakfast. The hotel supports Sala Baï School which trains young Cambodians for careers in the hospitality industry. It also partners with Naga Biofuels, a local NGO that produces clean-burning biodiesel recycled from used cooking oil.

Jasmine Lodge

National Road #6, 307 Taphul Village
phone: 012 784 980
www.jasminelodge.com
$

A small friendly guesthouse run by a local Cambodian family. A large selection of affordable rooms ranging from basic to deluxe are available. Enjoy dining in their upstairs restaurant and bar and sip a beer while playing a game of pool. Book exchange, DVDs and music are available. Jasmine offers tours to local charitable organizations and accepts clothing, book and supplies donations for those charities.

Jaya House River Park

River Road
phone: 063 962 555
www.jayahouseriverparksiemreap.com
$$$$

Thirty-six rooms, two pools, set along the Siem Reap River, about a six-minute tuk-tuk ride from town. Rooms include wi-fi and a complimentary mini-bar with a selection of homegrown teas and an espresso machine. Jaya House supports several NGOs, including Green Gecko helping street kids and their families.

La Residence Blanc D'Angkor

#194 Krous Village
Svay Dangkum and 6th Street
phone: 063 963 332
www.residenceblancangkor.com
$$

Boutique hotel with 26 contemporary rooms and several common living areas designed by a Cambodian architect. Double, twin, and family rooms with private balconies overlooking palm and coconut trees. Breakfast and airport transfers included. The hotel provides employment opportunities to students at Journeys Within Our Community, an educational NGO. Seventy-percent of the hotel's staff are Khmer students.

Mad Monkey Backpackers Hostel

Sivatha Road
phone: 063 688 0008
www.madmonkeyhostels.com
$ - $$

Room for 100 guests in A/C private rooms, shared double and dorm rooms. Pillows and bedding provided. Swimming pool and rooftop beach bar. Strict no-drugs or sex tourism policies. Mad Monkey works with local partners on socially-responsible projects such as its Crawl for School program that supports kids' educational costs, and a project focused on building clean water wells.

Paul Dubrule Hotel and Tourism School

National Road #6
On the way to the airport, near Airport Rd,
4 km from town
phone: 063 963 672
www.ecolepauldubrule.org
$ - $$

Four lovely rooms set in beautiful gardens each with AC, private bath, TV and minibar. Laundry service and airport transport are provided. The Paul Dubrule School (NGO), provides underprivileged young Cambodians with high-quality hospitality training that meets both international standards and the needs of local employers in the hotel, restaurant and tourism industry.

Rosy Guesthouse

#74 East River Road
Opposite the Royal Gardens
phone: 063 965 059
www.rosyguesthouse.com
$ - $$

Family-run guesthouse with 13 rooms (9 en suite and 4 shared bathrooms) in a French colonial-style Khmer villa. Rooms are equipped with wi-fi, cable TV, DVD players and air conditioning and/or fans. Strict policy against sex tourism. Rosy supports several NGOs, is active in environmental issues, and provides interest-free loans to its staff for hospital expenses, bicycle or motorbike repair or purchase, school fees, etc.

Sala Bai Hotel and Restaurant School

On Wat Svay - Tonle Sap Road
Head south toward Tonle Sap Lake
Near Wat Svay Primary School
phone: 063 963 329
www.salabai.com
$ - $$

A hotel and catering school for disadvantaged young Cambodians. Three simple but tastefully decorated rooms and one suite are available, all with AC and hot water.

Shinta Mani Hotel

Junction of Oum Khun and Street 14
phone: 063 761 998
www.shintamani.com
$$$ - $$$$

Shinta Mani, which in Sanskrit, means "The gem that provides everything one desires," is an intimate and elegant 18-room boutique hotel. The hotel runs the Institute of Hospitality Institute for orphaned and underprivileged young Cambodians. Guests are offered the opportunity to meet and sponsor students of the Institute and participate in the local community.

Soria Moria Boutique Hotel

Wat Bo Road
phone: 063 964 768
www.thesoriamoria.com
$$ - $$$

A unique experience of traditional Khmer hospitality and Scandinavian sophistication, with an enthusiastic approach to responsible and sustainable tourism practices. The hotel features deluxe rooms, a rooftop bar, sky jacuzzi (cold), sun deck, spa and wireless internet. Soria Moria supports NEDO, The White Bicycles, Love Cards, Sangkheum Center for Children, The Iron Workshop, Angkor Hospital for Children, Green Gecko, ChildSafe and The Silk Lab.

Templation Hotel

Rok Rak Street
phone: 092 783 622
www. maads.asia/templation
$$$$

Thirty-three suites and villas set among lush gardens. All villas have private pools, while the suites have their own terraces. Has a restaurant, bar and lounge. Complimentary breakfast. Templation Spa collaborates with Bodia, a renowned line of spa treatments and nature-based oils and lotions, inspired by traditional healing in Cambodia. Their shop carries exclusive locally-made handicraft, jewelry, gifts, swimwear and a selection of trendy clothing. The hotel is committed to responsible and sustainable tourism.

The Villa Siem Reap

153 Taphul Road
phone: 063 761 036
www.thevillasiemreap.com
$ - $$$

Rooms to suit any budget, all immaculately clean, with AC, minibar, TV, in-room safe and some rooms with a private garden and balcony. Free wireless internet access is available in the restaurant and on the balconies. The Villa actively promotes its own Water Filter Project and Give Blood Project, as well as White Bikes, Love Cards, Ibis Rice, ACCB. 7% of all profits are donated to charities in Siem Reap. They are committed to staff development and welfare. "Sex tourists are not welcome" is hotel policy.

Restaurants

Blossom Café

#6 Mondul
Behind Siem Reap Hospital
phone: 017 800 301
www.blossomcakes.org

Beautiful cakes and a café run by a not-for-profit organization that empowers and skills underprivileged Cambodian women and trafficking survivors while providing you with a chic oasis to unwind. Fair trade coffee, cupcakes, greeting cards.

Butterflies Garden Restaurant

Across the river from the Old Market in the Wat Bo area. Cross the Siem Reap River. Take a hard left and continue north along the river until you reach the next bridge. Turn right and continue 50 meters to the restaurant.
phone: 063 761 211
www.butterfliesofangkor.com
6am to 10pm

Superb dining in a garden restaurant with butterflies flitting among flowering plants and fruiting trees. The restaurant's goal is to help build a promising future for disadvantaged youth in Siem Reap. In addition, the gift shop now sources 80% of items directly from disadvantaged groups including families living with HIV/AIDS, widows and persons with disabilities.

Common Grounds

#719-21 Street 14
Near Angkor Hospital for Children
Phone: 063 965 687
www.commongroundscafes.org
7:30am to 8pm Monday to Friday

An American-style coffee house and cyber café serving great hot, cold and frozen coffee drinks and more. Their menu includes; cappuccino, latte, espresso, tea, fresh fruit smoothies, croissants, cookies, tarts, cake, soup, sandwiches, salads, omelets, Asian dishes and more. It is a place to relax, check your email (free wireless Internet) and meet locals and fellow travelers in a comfortable and modern atmosphere. Employees are hired locally and profits are reinvested into humanitarian relief projects in Cambodia.

Haven

Chocolate Rd
Wat Damnak area
phone: 078 342 404
www.haven-cambodia.com
11:30am to 2:30pm and 5:30pm to 9:30pm

A social enterprise and training restaurant for young adults from orphanages, safe shelters and poor rural areas. The Cambodia chef visits the market daily for fresh, MSG-free ingredients. Traditional Khmer dishes and unusual vegetarian fare such as eggplant and beet sandwiches and pumpkin burgers.

Joe to Go Restaurant

Street 9
Near the Old Market
phone: 098 939 066
www.joetogo.org
7am to 9:30pm, daily

Joe to Go offers coffee and meals. Smoothies, shakes, and traditional dishes such as fish amok and fried Cambodian noodles. All profits go the Global Child, a school for former street working children.

Kroya Restaurant

Junction of Om Khun and Street 14
In Shinta Mani Hotel, by the Post Office
phone: 063 761 998
www.shintamani.com/club/
food-beverage/kroya/
6am to 10:30 am Breakfast buffet,
Noon to 2:30pm Lunch, 2:30pm to 4:30pm
Tea, 6 pm to 10:30pm Dinner

Offering elegant indoor dining and casual
yet upscale terrace dining featuring both
Khmer and Western style cuisine. The
menu is a contemporary take on Asian and
international styles utilizing local organic
ingredients with quality imported products.
The Institute of Hospitality provides free
training for young Cambodians at risk.

Le Jardin des Delices (Paul Dubrule Hotel and Tourism School)

National Road #6
On the way to the airport, near Airport Road
4 km from town
phone: 089 629 398
www.ecolepauldubrule.org
12 noon to 2pm, Tuesday - Friday

Le Jardin des Delices is a student-training
restaurant, set in an exotic garden. The
restaurant serves a set three-course meal
for lunch and is open to the public. The
Paul Dubrule School (NGO) provides
underprivileged young Cambodians with
high-quality hospitality training that meets
both international standards and the needs
of local employers in the hotel, restaurant and
tourism industry. All income contributes to the
self-financing of their educational project.

Marum

#8 Phum Slokram
Between Wat Polanka and Catholic Church
phone: 017 363 284
www.friends-international.org
11am to 11pm, daily

Creative local cuisine, delicious cocktails and
fruit shakes, made using only the freshest
ingredients. Start with goat cheese fresh
spring rolls, then enjoy grilled sea bass and
smoky eggplant or prawn and mango stir fry,
and finish with chocolate Kampot pepper
cake. One of the Friends NGO training
programs that helps street children.

New Leaf Café

#306 Street 9
Near the Old Market
phone: 063 766 016
www.newleafeatery.com
7:30am to 7:30pm, daily

"Taste of Cambodia" high quality dining.
Locally source and environmentally
conscious. Run by a non-profit. Also sells fair-
trade crafts. Supports educational programs
in the Siem Reap area, which remains very
poor despite the thriving tourist trade.

Peace Café

East River Road
Next to Prah Ann Kau Saa Pagoda.
phone: 063 965 210
www.peacecafeangkor.org
8am to 9pm

A relaxing café, set in a spacious garden, serving fresh and healthy vegetarian meals. Peace Café offers vegetarian cooking classes, free space for community activities, a child-friendly garden and informative presentations on development projects, environmental issues and volunteer opportunities. Weekly yoga, pilates, tai chi and meditation classes, monk chats, live music, movies, bocce and table tennis, free internet and wireless access.

Sala Bai Hotel and Restaurant School

On Wat Svay - Tonle Sap Road
Head south toward Tonle Sap Lake
Near Wat Svay Primary School
phone: 063 963 329
www.salabai.com/restaurant-salabai.php
7am to 9am and 12 to 2pm Monday to Friday,
7:30am to 9:30am on weekends

A hotel and catering school that trains 100 young disadvantaged Cambodians each year. The comprehensive training program

lasts 11 months and includes 4½ months of internship. The training hotel and restaurant is open to the public to allow students to practice in real conditions. Enjoy a set menu of Western or Cambodian cuisine and a full range of drinks.

Sister Srey Café

200 Pokambor Avenue
Riverside and Old Market area
phone: 097 723 8001
www.sistersreycafe.com
7am to 6pm

Sister Srey is a social enterprise operated by two sisters (srey means sister in Khmer) to help students trying to balance their studies with work to support their families. Staff are trained in hospitality, English skills, personal development, health and hygiene and banking. Menu is gluten-free, vegan and vegetarian friendly.

Soria Moria Fusion Kitchen

Wat Bo Road
phone: 063 964 768
www.thesoriamoria.com/facilities
Lunch and dinner daily

Serving a selection of local delicacies as well as Scandinavian and Japanese specialties. The rooftop bar serves refreshing cocktails and tropical fruit shakes. Soria Moria supports NEDO, The White Bicycles, Love Cards, Sangkheum Center for Children, The Iron Workshop, Angkor Hospital for Children, Green Gecko, ChildSafe and The Silk Lab.

The Steakhouse at Pub Street

Pub Street
between The Passage and Street 9
phone: 063 965 501
www.shintamani.com/resort/food-beverage/the-steak-house-at-pub-street
6pm - 11pm

An American steakhouse featuring prime cuts of grilled beef, abundant side dishes and an excellent selection of wine and cocktails. The Shinta Mani Foundation is a leader in responsible tourism. Employs staff from their hospitality training program for young Cambodians at-risk. Funds community development.

Craft Shops

Artisans d'Angkor

Stung Thmey Street
Close to the Old Market
phone: 063 963 330
www.artisansdangkor.com
7:30am to 5:30pm, daily

Cambodian fine arts and crafts made by in-house artisans are displayed their showroom. The Angkor Craft Center offers free guided tours of the workshops to view stone and wood carving, lacquering and silk painting. The workshop is a training program for rural youth and the disabled learning artisan skills.

AKA Fair Trade Village

Road 60
On the way to the Angkor Wat Ticket Booth
200 meters after the bridge
phone: 078 341 454
www.aha-kh.com

Angkor Handicraft Association is a non-profit that aims to strengthen the handicraft sector and improve the quality of life for thousands of local artisans. Eighty percent of the souvenirs sold in town are imported or mass produced and most travelers are unable to identify authentic products. AKA Fair Trade Village has stalls with local handmade art and souvenirs.

Friends 'n' Stuff (2 locations)

First location: at Marum Restaurant
#8 Phum Slokram
between Wat Polanka and the
Catholic Church
11am to 10:30pm, daily
Second location: Made In Cambodia
Market in Shinta Mani Resort
At Oum Khun and 14th Street
4pm to 9 pm on Saturday, Sunday
and Tuesday
www.friendsnstuff.org

Colorful shop offering a wide range of products made by Friends International (NGO) students in training and by parents of former street children. Purses, clothing, necklaces, handbags and recycled products.

Institute of Khmer Textiles Shop

Tonle Sap Rd
Half a kilometer south of Old Market
phone: 063 964 437
www.ikttearth.org

Traditional ikat silk weaving was revived by this Japanese NGO and is now a self-sustaining community of 160 people. Visit the beautiful gift shop and workshop. Their village, where they harvest dye products from the forest, is an hour away and has a guest house.

Mekong+

#5 Sivatha Boulevard
phone: 063 964 498
www.mekong-plus.com

Hand-crafted quilts and accessories. A social enterprise creating sustainable employment for under-privileged rural women.

Sao Mao

2nd of December Street
Across from the Old Market by Sivatha Boulevard
phone: 063 761 224
www.saomao.com
8am to 9pm

A socially responsible business practicing equitable finance and working to make a difference in the lives of Cambodian people. Sao Mao works with village producers and artisans, assisting and advising in design and product development and promoting both traditional and contemporary crafts and design.

Three Seasons

between Streets 7 and 8
phone: 012 414 596
www.elsewhere2.asia

Local fashion at its best. Cambodian-made designs, clothes & accessories. Owners are committed to responsible tourism.

Arts & Culture

Artisans d'Angkor

Stung Thmey Street
Close to the Old Market
phone: 063 963 330
www.artisansdangkor.com/workshops-18-siem-reap-workshops.php
8am to 5pm, daily

The Angkor Craft Center offers free guided tours of the workshops to view stone and wood carving, lacquering and silk painting. The workshop is a training program for rural youth and the disabled to learn artisan skills. The artisan's products are displayed in the boutique.

Artisans d'Angkor Silk Farm
(Puok District)

Centre National de la Soie (CNS)
20 minutes from Siem Reap
phone: 099 555 109
www.artisansdangkor.com
7am to 5pm, daily

An informative free guided tour of the silk farm. See artisans at work in each step of the traditional silk-making process and walk among the mulberry tree groves that provide food for silkworms. A shuttle bus is provided free of charge from Artisans d'Angkor at 9:30am and 1:30pm.

Chili Pepper Restaurant

Siem Reap River Street
North of National Road #6
Located at Kafu Resort
7:30pm on Wednesdays

NGO Krousar Thmey's children perform traditional music, dance and shadow puppets performances. All proceeds from the show are directly donated back to Krousar Thmey and help support the children, the center and all of its programs.

Le Tigre de Papier Cooking School and Restaurant

On Pub Street
phone: 012 265 811
www.letigredepapier.com/en/cooking.php
In English at 10am and 1pm;
in French and English at 5pm

A Cambodian cooking class includes a trip to the local market with the Chef to shop for lunch ingredients, followed by a cooking lesson and a delicious meal. The restaurant supports Sala Bai Hotel and Restaurant School, an organzation that trains young disadvantaged Cambodians.

Peace Café

East River Road
Next to Prah Ann Kau Saa Pagoda.
phone: 063 965 210
www.peacecafeangkor.org/program.htm
8am to 9pm

Offering weekly monk chats, meditation, yoga, Pilates, tai chi, vegetarian cooking classes, performances and talks. Peace Café offers free space for community activities, a child-friendly garden, informative presentations on development projects and environmental issues and information on volunteer opportunities.

Phare Circus

Phare Circus Ring Road
South of the intersection with Sok San Road
phone: 092 225 320
www.pharecircus.org

Shows are inspired by the real-life experiences of Phare's creators and performers who use music, dance, theater and circus arts to deal with themes such as war, discrimination, relationships and poverty. No circus animals.

The Cambodia Landmine Museum

6 km south of Banteay Srey Temple on the main road from town. About 30 - 40 minutes from Siem Reap.
www.cambodialandminemuseum.org
7:30am to 5:30pm, daily
5 USD admission

An informative and thought-provoking landmine museum. The facility provides a home and education for young landmine survivors and at-risk youth. The founder's dramatic personal story demonstrates great courage.

Tonle Sap Exhibition

On the road to Angkor Wat just past the Jayavarman VII hospital
phone: 063 964 694 or 023 366 184
www.krousar-thmey.org/en/our-work/culturel-artistic-development/
8:00am to 12:00pm and
1:30pm to 5:30pm, daily
Donations accepted

The exhibit features Tonle Sap Lake and the local people, culture and environment. Informative displays, maps, photos, models of traditional houses, boats and fishing implements with written explanations in French, English and Khmer. Sponsored by Krousar Thmey, an NGO assisting deprived children in Cambodia.

Massage & Services

Krousar Thmey Massage

On the road to Angkor Wat just past the Jayavarman VII hospital at the Tonle Sap Exhibition
phone: 063 964 694 or 023 366 184
www.krousar-thmey.org
8am to 8pm, daily

Relaxing massages given by blind Cambodian specialists. Sponsored by Krousar Thmey, an NGO assisting deprived children in Cambodia.

Phka Kravan Beauty Salon

Take Sivatha Boulevard south,
cross Pokambor St at the roundabout,
Phka Kravan is on the right.
phone: 092 814 841
Facebook @Phka Kravan

Where Beauty Changes Life... a training salon for hair and nails that gives Khmer youth the opportunity to develop skills in the beauty industry. Run by Friends International.

Seeing Hands 4 Massage by the Blind

324 Sivatha Boulevard
25m behind Cambodia Commercial Bank
phone: 012 786 894

Seeing Hands 411 Massage by the Blind

Located on the street opposite the CAB
phone: 012 286 316

Massage and shiatsu by blind professionals. Effective for relief of stress and for relaxation. Cool and comfortable atmosphere with quiet music.

Meditation

Wat Bo Meditation and Conversation

Wat Bo Road
phone: 012 756 490
4 to 5pm

The monks at Wat Bo offer free Buddhist meditation sessions and hold informal conversation sessions about Buddhism and their daily life.

Eco-tours

Gecko Environment Center

Main Siem Reap port, Phnom Krom, Chong Khneas Commune
By road during the wet season and by car and boat during the dry season
phone: 063 963 525
jinja.apsara.org/gecko/
8:30am to 5pm, daily, Free

A floating environmental center located in Siem Reap Province on the Tonle Sap lake. The center practices sustainable natural resource management using interactive environmental education activities with communities around the lake. The center also features displays and information on local flora, fauna and traditional community activities for visitors.

Osmose

phone: 063 965 574
www.osmosetonlesap.net
80 USD

Tonle Sap Lake tours focusing on the links between conservation, ecotourism, environmental education and sustainable development. Since 1999, Osmose has undertaken a pilot action linking conservation and development in the Prek Toal area of the Tonle Sap Lake. The site is the last breeding stronghold in Southeast Asia for large water birds, which were once seriously threatened by massive egg and chick collection for local consumption. The project implements an original approach integrating water bird conservation, environmental education and ecotourism, with the equitable development of the local communities as an overall goal. After six years of efforts, the water bird colonies have been saved, more than 1000 children have participated in the environmental education program and over 100 poor families benefit from socio-sanitary support and alternative income-generating activities.

KKO Bike Tour

Wat Bo Road and Street 20
phone: 093 903 024
www.kko-cambodia.org

Off-road bicycle tours to the Angkor temples; sunrise and sunset tours; countryside tours; and motorbike tours to Cambodian villages. Proceeds support Khmer for Khmer's free English classes and free vocational training in motorbike mechanics. 30-50 USD for bicycle tours.

PURE! Countryside Bike Tour

Hup Guan Street
phone: 086 975 425
www.puredreamcentre.org

Half-day tours (17 kilometers) with an English-speaking guide that take in local life around Siem Reap, including a market and lunch with a local family. Proceeds support PURE's educational and vocational-training projects for disadvantaged children. 25-35 USD

Sam Veasna Center

Off Wat Bo Road by Angkor Village Hotel, 250 meters on right
phone: 063 96 37 10
www.samveasna.org

In partnership with Wildlife Conservation Society (WCS), Sam Veasna Center arranges itineraries and day trips to key bird sites across Cambodia, using local information from WCS rangers to locate flagship species. Their objective is to provide alternative sustainable livelihoods from ecotourism for local communities using no hunting and land conversion agreements.

Birding with Sam Veasna Center

I like bird watching so much that I usually read a guide to the birds of the region I'm visiting. On my first trip to Cambodia, I was in a tour bus and glimpsed only a few birds. The most frustrating thing was that I kept reading about how common bee eaters were, but I still hadn't seen one. On my second trip, I was there during migration season and signed up for a day-long birding tour to Tonle Sap Lake with Sam Veasna Center. Not only did we see Open-billed Storks, Black-headed Ibises, Anhingas, Lesser Adjutants and the highlight of the tour, Painted Storks, but also I got to see the highlight of my trip, the Blue-tailed Bee Eater!

Shoshana Kerewsky

Sihanoukville

Kbal Chhay
Waterfall

Ferry to
Koh Kong

National Road No 4

National Road No 4

Victory Beach
(North)

Victory Beach
(South)
Hawaii Beach

Victory
Monument

Independence
Square

See
Detail
Map

Independence
Hotel

Don Bosco [H]
Hotel & Restaurant

Independence
Beach

Sadan [R]

Sokha Beach

Cambodian Children's
Painting Project
and M'Lop Tapang Shop

Ocheuteal
Beach

Otres
Beach

| [H] Hotel | [R] Restaurant | [A] Arts & Culture |
| [C] Craft Shop | [m] Massage | [T] Transportation |

Sihanoukville

Sihanoukville (pop: 89,800) is blessed with palm fringed, white sandy beaches. These can be a welcome reprieve from the busy cities, temple crowds and rough roads. Be like the Cambodians by enjoying a picnic in the shade overlooking the ocean, then taking a nap in a hammock, or treat yourself to a walk on a sandy beach and a swim in the balmy sea. Try some of the abundant and delectable fresh seafood, or take an excursion to nearby islands.

Itinerary Highlights

Day 1

- Relax at the beach in the morning.
- Have lunch at Starfish Restaurant, check your email and get a massage by Sala Santepeap Massage Centre or Seeing Hands.
- Enjoy a fresh seafood dinner on the beach at sunset.

Day 2

- Explore Ream National Park on an all-day boat trip and nature tour with a naturalist.
- Relax again at the beach, watch the sunset while sipping a cold fresh coconut juice.

Where to Stay

Don Bosco Hotel School

Ou Pram Street/Otres Road past the market
2.5km down Otres Rd from Psa Lue Market.
Right at the Don Bosco School sign
phone: 034 934 478
www.donboscohotelschool.com
$$ - $$$

A hotel school and accommodations
dedicated to educating Cambodian youth
in need. Stylish, quiet, clean rooms with
AC, cable TV, internet, mini-bar, fridge
and phone. Facilities include a swimming
pool, restaurant and large conference room
on spacious landscaped grounds. Airport,
bus station or ferry-dock pick up and
complimentary shuttles to the main beaches
are provided.

The Small Hotel

Located in the city center behind
the Caltrex Station
phone: 034 630 6161
$ - $$

A quiet little hotel off the main road in the
center of town. Featuring large, clean rooms
with TV, mini-bar, fan, AC and hot water.

A small bar/restaurant serves breakfast,
western dishes, Swedish specialties and a
few Asian dishes. The hotel supports Help
the Cambodian Children, an organization
that builds schools, provides education,
recreational facilities, health care and
opportunities for learning job skills. A
ChildSafe member.

Restaurants

Don Bosco Hotel School Restaurant

Ou Pram Street /Otres Road past the market
2.5km down Otres Rd from Psa Lue Market.
Right at the Don Bosco School sign
phone: 034 934 478
www.donboscohotelschool.com

Hotel school, restaurant and accommodations dedicated to educating
Cambodian youth in need. The restaurant
and large conference room overlook the pool,
on spacious landscaped grounds.

Ristorante Gelato Italiano

Located in a new building near
the Tourism Office
phone: 034 934 672
www.donboscohotelschool.com

A downtown restaurant serving espresso
drinks, breakfast, pizza and snacks. The
main attraction is the authentic Italian ice
cream, made by the Don Bosco Hotel School
students using natural ingredients and fresh
fruit. The school is dedicated to educating
Cambodian youth in need.

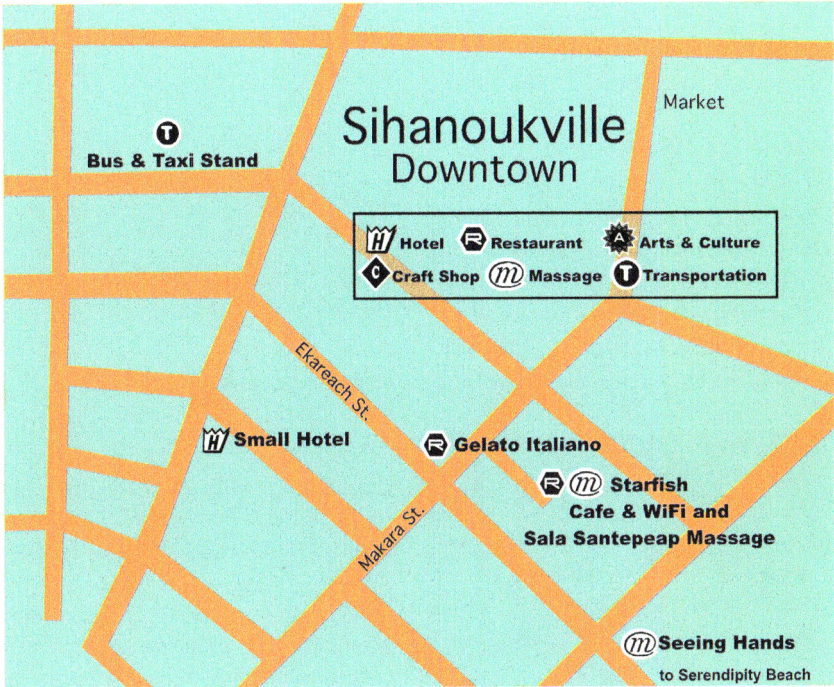

Bus & Taxi Stand

Sihanoukville
Downtown

Market

H Hotel **R** Restaurant **A** Arts & Culture	
C Craft Shop **m** Massage **T** Transportation	

Ekareach St.

H Small Hotel

R Gelato Italiano

R **m** **Starfish Cafe & WiFi and Sala Santepeap Massage**

Makara St.

m **Seeing Hands**

to Serendipity Beach

After spending time at the beach, wander downtown and enjoy homemade gelato.

Sandan

On the road to Sokha Beach
100m from the Golden Lions Circle
phone: 034 452 4000
www.friends-international.org
11am to 10pm, daily

Delicious Khmer food that comes highly recommended. Indoor and outdoor seating. A training program for disadvantaged youth age 15 and up. Staff are warm and attentive. Run by M'Lop Tapang, an NGO that helps street children.

Starfish Bakery and Café

Downtown behind Sumudera Supermarket, off Makara Street
phone: 012 952 011
www.starfishcambodia.org
7am to 6pm, daily

Enjoy healthy western-style lunches and delicious coffee, home-baked bread, cookies, brownies and fresh fruit shakes in a lush garden environment. The Starfish Project (NGO) employs individuals with physical disabilities to help them and their families become independent. Projects involve medical and livelihood assistance, community and water projects and housing.

Craft Shops

Cambodian Children's Painting Project (CCPP)

Ochheuteal Beach
Down the dirt road to Serenity Beach
phone: 017 500 402
www.letuscreate.org

Committed to providing a cultural and social platform for the beach children of Sihanoukville. NGO CCPP's goal is to give children a safe environment, a chance to develop their imagination and skills through artistic painting as a core activity and to generate some basic income for themselves and their family needs through the sale of their paintings. CCPP also supports the children to pursue regular schooling by helping connect artistic expression to their general education.

M'Lop Tapang Shop

Down the dirt road to Serenity Beach
phone: 043 934 072
www.mloptapang.org

An NGO gift shop offering support to the street children of Sihanoukville. The children are offered regular meals, shelter, medical care, education, counseling and protection from abuse. Their goal is to provide a safe haven for the street children of Sihanoukville and to help them reintegrate into their families and community.

Internet

Starfish Wireless Internet Centre

In the Starfish Bakery & Café, downtown behind Sumudera Supermarket
phone: 012 952 011
www.starfishcambodia.org

Keep in touch with friends and family at the Internet center set in the relaxing greenery of the café. The Starfish Project (NGO) employs individuals with physical disabilities to help them and their families become independent. Projects involve medical and livelihood assistance, community and water projects and housing.

Massage

Sala Santepeap Massage Centre

Inside Starfish Bakery & Café, downtown behind Sumudera Supermarket
phone: 012 952 011
www.starfishcambodia.org

Relax with an Indian head massage, neck and back, Thai, aromatherapy or foot massage provided by experienced blind masseurs. Run by the Starfish Project (NGO), employing individuals with physical disabilities to help them and their families become independent. Projects involve medical and livelihood assistance, community and water projects and housing.

Seeing Hands 3

Ekareach Street
Near Holy Cow
phone: 012 799 016
6 USD

A massage center by the blind. Japanese-style Anma and shiatsu to release stress and tension.

Kampot

to
Phnom
Penh
148 KM

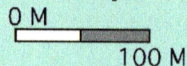

0 M   100 M

National Highway 3

Market

Street 714

Street 716

Street 729

Street 718

Street 720

Hospital

to Bokor 40 KM

Old Bridge Street

to Sihanoukville 105 KM

Street 722

Riverside Road

Shared Taxi Stand T

Street 701

Street 705

Street 707

Epic Arts R

C
Dorsu: Made In Cambodia

m **Seeing Hands**

Street 730

728
R
H **Rikitikitavi**

Street 701

H **Hotel**	R **Restaurant**	A **Arts & Culture**
C **Craft Shop**	m **Massage**	T **Transportation**

H **Mad Monkey**

Kampot

Kampot (pop: 39,200) is a quiet and charming provincial capital with classic French colonial and Chinese architecture. The town is located on the Teuk Chhou River with panoramic views of Bokor and Elephant Mountains. Its relaxing pace can be a welcome relief if you are coming from Phnom Penh. Kampot is renowned for its black pepper and you will find it in many of the locally prepared dishes.

Itinerary Highlights

Day 1

- Walk or take a boat down the river, explore nearby caves, or visit the beach town of Kep and its surrounding islands. Stop by Epic Arts Café for a respite and get a snack. Watch the sunset at Little Garden Restaurant and enjoy a cold fruit smoothie or cocktail.

Day 2

- Visit Bokor National Park or volunteer at one of the local organizations. Get a massage at Seeing Hands. Enjoy the river breezes at sunset while savoring a fine dinner at Rikitikitavi.

Where to Stay

Mad Monkey Backpackers Hostel

Riverside Rd
phone: 096 872 6525
www.madmonkeyhostels.com
$-$$

Room for 72 guests in with a variety of options from dorms to private rooms. Pool and restaurant. Strict no-drugs or sex tourism policies. An educational aid fund helps develop facilities, buy school equipment and fund transportation

Kampot

Rikitikitavi

River Road
By Bokor Mountain Lodge
phone: 012 235 102
www.rikitikitavi-kampot.com
$$

A boutique guesthouse offering a small and personal selection of rooms that are decorated in a modern Asian style. Rooms include AC, fan, hot shower, cable TV and DVD player. Rikitikitavi treats staff with respect, trains them and provides the best wages and maintains a quality work environment. They discuss child safety issues with their staff and maintain a zero tolerance towards child prostitution. On their website, information is provided on a wide variety of local issues including cultural and social topics. Rikitikitavi uses local trades people and other local businesses as much as possible.

Restaurants

Epic Arts Café

#67 Oosaupia Mouy
Near the Old Market and Mealy Chenda
phone: 012 376 968
www.epicarts.org.uk/programme/epic-cafe/
7am to 6pm, daily

A project providing opportunities to the deaf and disabled communities. Teas, cakes, shakes, lunch and snacks are all on the menu. Epic Arts' focus is on changing people's attitudes towards disability, encouraging the belief that every person can make a contribution to their community. Art performance is used as a key means to encourage the general community to involve disabled people in the arts and other

areas of work and to view them as valued members of society.

Rikitikitavi

River Road
By Bokor Mountain Lodge
phone: 012 235 102
www.rikitikitavi-kampot.com

A beautifully designed terrace restaurant overlooking the Tek Chou River with the Elephant Mountains as a backdrop. The restaurant serves fine foods made with the freshest quality ingredients. The menu includes an all day breakfast menu, well-packed sandwiches that are ideal for day trips including the BLT Melt and Cracked Pepper Chicken (with genuine Kampot pepper). More selections include delicious finger foods, Chicken Yogurt Wraps, Eggplant Parmagiana, Steak and Guinness Pie, Chicken Satay and Spaghetti Carbonara. The nearly famous apple pie also makes a fantastic (even if naughty) lunch. See their responsible business practices above in their hotel description.

Shopping

Dorsu: Made in Cambodia

#35 Street 724
Northside of Old Market
phone: 012 960 225
www.dorsu.org
10am to 7pm, daily

Contemporary fashion. Setting the standard for fair and ethical treatment of employees and a safe work environment. Supports a Cambodian NGO serving the local community.

Visiting Buddhist Temples & Spirit Altars

Buddhism - *95% of Cambodia's population is Buddhist. Buddhism as practiced in Cambodia is the cultural foundation for daily living. Each city has many Buddhist temples where orange-robed monks reside. In the morning, the monks can be seen going from house to house with their begging bowls collecting cooked rice and other food. People want to help the monks because the merit they earn will help them in their next life. Tourists are welcome to contribute money to the monks or at the temple and will be blessed with a chanted prayer.*

The two major holidays, Cambodian New Year (mid-April) and Ancestors Remembrance Day (end of September), involve taking food and gifts to the monks in the temple. Devoted Buddhists will also take food to the temple on the full moon and new moon. This is a nice time to visit the temple to see the activities. Be sure to dress modestly, with shoulders and legs covered, arrive before 11 am, take off your shoes before entering, put some money in the donation box, sit down and enjoy the peaceful ambiance.

Animism - *This earth-based spirituality was the religion before Buddhism was introduced and it still is a part of most Cambodians' belief system. Many rural families have an altar in front of their house for the spirit that protect them and the house. They make offerings of incense, flowers and water. If you drive from Phnom Penh to Sihannoukville you will see people stopping mid-way at a long line of altars, to pray to for safe travels. If you are inclined to do so, you can stop, buy some incense and participate.*

Massage

Seeing Hands 3

Across from Bokor Mountain Lodge
phone: 012 328 465
6 USD

Massage center by the blind. Japanese-style Anma and shiatsu to release stress and tension.

Outlying Provinces

Banteay Meanchey

Sisophon Community-Based Tourism Office

National Road #56A
Banteay Chhmar Commune,
Thmor Puok District
phone: 097 516 5533
www.visitbanteaychhmar.org

Provides income for the local community by arranging a variety of services and experiences including guides for Bantey Chhmar temple ruins. Stay in comfortable award-winning fully-furnished tent cabins next to the ruins and enjoy dinner by candle light with live music. Also offers home-stays, village tours, birdwatching trips, boat rides, musical performances, ox-cart rides and Khmer-style dance lessons.

Battambang

Bamu Boutique Resort

Street 203
Three blocks from the river
phone: 053 953 900
www.bambuhotel.com

Sixteen-room boutique hotel in four traditionally-inspired buildings. Salt-water swimming pool. Breakfast included. The owners support a grass-roots school project in a nearby village where children use classrooms after hours to study English. Guests are invited to visit the school and help out in classroom. Member of ChildSafe.

Circus

Anch Anh Village
On Route #5 one km west of town
phone: 077 554 413
www.phareps.org
7pm on Thursday
call for other scheduled performances

Traditional Cambodian circus acts performed by the students of the Circus School. In partnership with Asian Trails, Phare Ponleu Selpak (NGO) gives Cambodian children from poor and disabled families the opportunity to have access to culture via artistic activities, including music, drawing, drama, dancing and circus.

Fresh Eats Café

#47 Pub Street
South of Psar Nat (Central Market)
phone: 012 88 1784
www.mpkhomeland.org

Western and Khmer dishes made with local and organic ingredients. Part of a cooking school operated by Homeland, an NGO helping vulnerable children.

Green Orange Village Café, Guesthouse, and Kayaks

Ksach Poy Village
Wat Kor Commune, Svay Por District
phone: 012 718 857
www.fedacambodia.org

The Café uses local produce. Offers simple rooms in a guest house. Kayaks can be rented at the café – reserve in advance. The journey along the Sangke River to Battambang city center takes about two hours (11 kilometers) and is an excellent way to discover the way of life of local people as you gently paddle down the river and enjoy the scenes unfold before you. A project of Friends Economic Development Association (FEDA), a NGO alleviating poverty by empowering rural people. Opportunities for international volunteers.

Jaan Bai Restaurant

Street 2
South of Psar Nat (Central Market)
phone: 078 263 144
www.cambodianchildrenstrust.org

Enjoy a seven course meal or a small plate. Rated one of the top restaurants in Battambang. They use seasonal organic produce sourced from local farmers and the kitchen garden at their community youth center. It is a training and employment program for youth in partnership with Cambodia Children's Trust, an Australian NGO.

Rachana Handicrafts

#97 Group 5 Prek Preah Sdach Village,
Prek Preah Sdach Commune,
Battambang District
phone: 012 940 358

An NGO shop selling silk and cotton accessories, purses, scarves and toys. Rachana trains disadvantaged women in sewing handicrafts, which helps them build self-confidence and contribute towards their families and community.

Kampong Speu

Chambok Community-Based Ecotourism Site

Off National Road #4
2 hours from Phnom Penh
on the way to Sihanoukville
www.chambok.org
phone: 010 730 600

Located near Kirirom National Park, Chambok offers beautiful hiking trails, bird watching, oxcart rides, bicycle rentals, and a 40-meter waterfall. You can learn how to make traditional crafts or you can sample Cambodian cuisine in their women-run restaurant, serving locally-sourced and freshly prepared food. You can spend the night with a local family in one of their homestays and immerse yourself in rural life, or take a 2 or 3 day trek with a local guide and camp out in the forest. Chambok serves as a model for community-based ecotourism in Cambodia. Local guides are available for tours in the area and all profits go back into the community to help protect the surrounding forestlands.

Kirirom Mountain Lodge

Located in Kirirom National Park
Off National Road #4
2 hours from Phnom Penh
on the way to Sihanoukville
phone: 092 490 216
www.kirirom.asia
Fresh-air nature get-away. Six beautiful guest rooms in a newly-restored chalet at 700 meters elevation in a cool hill resort. Enjoy walks, cycling (bike rentals available) and picnics in the dry pine forest. Restaurant serving Mediterranean and local food. Owners are committed to responsible tourism.

Kampong Thom

Khmer Village and Homestay

Khmer Village and Homestay
Som Rong Village, Baray District
Off National Road #6
120km from Phnom Penh toward Siem Reap
phone: 012 635 718
www.khmerhomestaybaray.com

Catch a glimpse of village life and the essence of Khmer lifestyle. Activities include an ox cart tour of the village and market, Khmer noodle making, weaving, fishing and walking on a nature trail.

Kep

Sothy's Pepper Farm

Near the coast
Contact for directions: sothy@
mykampotpepper.asia
phone: 088 951 3505
www.mykampotpepper.asia

Learn about world-famous Kampot pepper. This ecological family fruit and pepper farm with solar power gives tours and welcomes volunteers. Organic restaurant on-site.

Veranda Natural Resort

Kep Hillside Road
phone: 012 888 619
www.veranda-resort.asia

A boutique hotel with private rooms and villas atop Kep National Park, overlooking the Gulf of Thailand. Pool, on-site restaurant. Rooms with A/C, TV and free wi-fi. Breakfast buffet included. Veranda recently supported the building of a well for a local school garden used to generate income for the school.

Koh Kong

Chi Phat and Wildlife Alliance

17 km from Andoeng Teuk
Off Highway 48
www.chi-phat.org
phone: 035 675 6444
www.wildlifealliance.org

Wildlife Alliance's model program of community-based eco-tourism (CBET) in Chi Phat, a village in the Southern Cardamom Mountains. Eco-tourism reduces the community's reliance on illegal logging and the wild animal trade and provides much needed income to impoverished communities. Local people are now employed as guides leading trekking, mountain-biking, camping, and river boat tours through the wilderness. Villagers also operate homestays, guest houses, motorbike taxi services, and restaurants, giving visitors further insight into rural life in Cambodia. Local CBET members manage the project and are given ongoing training as they perform bookings, arrange itineraries, do accounting, and oversee community ranger patrols. A community waste management system has also been developed - one of the first in Cambodia.

Oasis Bungalow Resort

2 km from Koh Kong town
Off Hwy 48
Near the coast and Thai border
phone: 092 228 342
www.oasisresort.netkhmer.com
Five large luxury bungalows set round an infinity pool with views of the Cardamom Mountains. Take excursions to waterfalls, island beaches, or mangrove forests. Strict policy against sex tourists.

Kratie

Cambodian Rural Discovery Tours & Guesthouse

Street 3 in Kratie Town
phone: 099 834 353
www.crdtours.com

A social enterprise, CRD Tours provides visitors with unforgettable learning experiences and provides the community with sustainable income and eco-development projects. See Irrawaddy dolphins, waterfalls or the Mekong Turtle Center. Offers homestays, tours, boat trips, mountain biking, and volunteer opportunities. Guestrooms and meals available at the Le Tonle Tourism Training Center. CRD also guides tours in remote and beautiful Mondulkiri and Ratanakiri provinces.

Stung Treng

Mekong Blue Weaving Center & Shop

4 km west of Stung Treng town
Along the river road
phone: 012 609 730
www.mekongblue.com

A 455 km from Phnom Penh, on the Mekong River, an area known for dolphins and waterfalls. Stung Treng Women's Development Center is an NGO that helps break the cycle of poverty by offering programs in literacy and health education, vocational training and employment. You can visit the weaving center. Stay at the Le Tonle Tourism Training Centre, which offers 4 guest rooms.

Takeo

Meas Family Homestay

Off National Road #3
71 km south of Phnom Penh
2 km from the town of Ang Tasom
www.cambodianhomestay.com

Near Angkor Borei ancient ruins. Eleven rooms in a rural farming area. Meals are included. Opportunities to teach English at the local high school, learn to cook Khmer food, visit a weaving village, or harvest rice (December).

Phnom Tamao Wildlife Rescue Center

On National Road #2
One and an half hour drive from Phnom Penh
phone: 095 970 175
www.wildlifealliance.org/wildlife-phnom-tamao

Tours benefit the work of Wildlife Alliance, an NGO fighting the illegal wildlife trade in Cambodia. See rescued tigers, otters, leopards, bears and monkeys. Eighty percent are released back into the wild. Feed the elephants and baby monkeys. Also in the area are Tonle Bati Lake and the Phnom Tamao and Phnom Chisor temples. 15 USD

Responsible Volunteering in Cambodia

Volunteering can be a wonderful way to get to know people in Cambodia and to offer kindness and goodwill. There are several ways to volunteer, as well as a few things to be aware of.

The most precious skill you may have, that no native Cambodian can duplicate, is speaking English without a foreign accent. If English is your native tongue, helping students practice their English is a valuable contribution you can make. You will see many signs for English schools in Cambodia and you can stop by and offer to practice English with students. If you are staying in Cambodia for an extended period, you may be able to arrange to teach a class. These opportunities are plentiful and usually need to be set up once you are in country.

Many Cambodian boys from rural areas want an education but cannot afford to live in the city where the schools are, so they temporarily become Buddhist monks. They are able to live in the temple for free while they go to secondary school or university. This is the only way they can afford an education. Girls, unfortunately, do not have this option. Buddhist temples are open to visitors and it is highly probable that some of the monks would welcome the opportunity to practice speaking English with you.

If you would like a more structured volunteer opportunity and have 1-3 weeks to offer, you can join a group that has volunteer service trips, such as Habitat for Humanity and help build a house. If you are a health professional, there are agencies, such as Medical Teams International, that send teams of doctors, dentists and EMS professionals to Cambodia for short-term volunteer opportunities.

Volunteering has many potential benefits for all concerned. The best volunteer placements work with the local communities, helping them to implement projects that they have identified, supplementing their skills and resources and leaving the community better able to take care of itself after the volunteers have left. In contrast, inappropriate volunteering can undermine local people's confidence, impose the volunteer's agenda, increase dependency on outside help and create more problems than it solves.

Remember that you are a role model and ambassador for yourself and your home country. Set a good example at all times in the way you dress, your behavior and your time keeping.

A controversial topic related to volunteering is working with children. Most of the large international agencies helping children in Cambodia recommend that foreigners should not volunteer at orphanages and other agencies working with vulnerable children. There are several reasons for this policy:

1) Due to the high rate of sexual exploitation of children in Cambodia and the complete lack of background screening of volunteers, they feel it is best to protect children by not allowing foreigners to volunteer.

2) Children who have lost their parents need long-term care providers who are consistently there for them. The agencies feel that when the child meets someone who plays with them for some days or weeks, bonds with the child and then disappears, it re-wounds the child and may breakdown their ability to bond in the future.

3) The number of corrupt orphanages is extremely high in Cambodia. The people running these facilities use the children for their personal gain and pocket donations intended to help the children. It is very difficult for you to tell which ones are corrupt and which ones are not when you a) do not speak the language, b) are not there for a long period of time and c) do not have an impartial reference.

Some agencies are suitable for volunteers who want to work with children and we have listed a few of them in this directory.

Do not be surprised if most non-profit organizations tell you that they do not want short-term volunteers. They have found that the amount of staff time required to orient, train and supervise volunteers exceeds the benefit. Most agencies are only interested in volunteers who are willing to make a commitment of 6 – 12 months, cover their own expenses (airfare, room and board) and offer needed skills, such as grant writing, computer skills, etc.

Take time to think about your goal. If your goal is to have an experience abroad that makes a contribution while you are there, then volunteering is a good way to do that. If your main goal is to help people in Cambodia, then raising funds at home and donating the proceeds to a non-profit organization working in Cambodia might be a better choice, especially if the funds are used to empower Cambodians to help themselves and make long-term improvements in their lives.

Volunteer Opportunities

Battambang

Khmer New Generation Organization

www.kngocambodia.org
Located in Bospo Village
Odambang I Commune, Sangker District
10 minutes from Battambang City
phone: 092 790 597

An Australian NGO providing supplementary education to youth including English, computer classes and vocational training.

How can I help? Teach English. They prefer a one month commitment or more.

Kampong Chnnang

Global Student Outreach

www.gsocambodia.org
Located in Chankiek Village,
Kampong Tralach

Global Student Outreach is committed to improving the lives of children and families of rural Cambodia. They have teaching, community service projects and sustainable farming education placements in rural Cambodia. Adults live with a host-family. Students live at their facility. 250 USD for two weeks - room and board included. One to six weeks.

How can I help? Teaching volunteers work side-by-side with the local English teacher for hour long classes that take place up to three times a day, presenting lessons and coordinating activities. Farming volunteers involved with this project for short periods of time will be planting vegetables, watering plants, weeding gardens, cleaning animal enclosures. Volunteers who stay longer may be involved in setting up green houses, building natural animal housing, or harvesting honey.

Kampot

Chumkriel Language School

www.chumkriellanguageschool.org
phone: 089 256 400
Located near the town of Kampot

A Cambodian-operated grassroots organization providing English classes, computer workshops, public library, supplementary lessons, agricultural programs, a sports field, and creative arts activities.

How can I help? CLS values volunteers with experience in teaching (especially English as a Second Language), computer/IT support, library support, marketing, fund raising, administration and project management. One month minimum commitment.

Phnom Penh

Kantha Bopha Children's Hospitals

Kantha Bopha I: Street 240, off Street 19
www.beat-richner.ch
phone: 023 428 009

Kantha Bopha Foundation has five fully operating hospitals including a maternity ward for HIV-positive mothers. The Kantha Bopha Children's Hospitals match international standards and offer their services free of charge to Cambodian families. Blood donations accepted daily.

How can I help? Donate blood

Siem Reap

ConCERT

ConCERT has placed volunteers in and around Siem Reap since 2008. They can assist you in finding an appropriate volunteering experience and save you the time and effort of searching and contacting different organizations on your own. They have more than 20 local projects where they can place volunteers. These are well-run projects working closely with local people towards a better future for Cambodia. They have detailed knowledge of what is needed and will place you with a project your skills and interests match the need. ConCERT's goal is to ensure that your volunteering experience will be constructive and contribute towards the long term goals of the project and the local community it serves.

Angkor Hospital for Children

www.angkorhospital.org
Tep Vong Street
phone: 063 963409
Visitor Center hours: 8am to 5pm,
closed Sunday

A full service pediatric hospital providing free and immediate medical assistance to the underserved children of Siem Reap.

How can I help? Donate blood

The Green Gecko Project

www.greengeckoproject.org
phone: 077 757 420

The project supports over 70 children who previously lived and begged on the streets of Siem Reap. Green Gecko provides security, education, love and opportunities to these children through their formative years and into their adult lives, empowering them to achieve their full potential. The project also supports the children's families and the broader community through long term health, education and training initiatives.

How can I help? The focus of their volunteer program is on specialized creative skills. They invite anyone with an interest in proposing a workshop program to send

them an email outlining their idea to see if it will be suitable for the Green Gecko project. As many of the Green Gecko kids are young adults themselves now, they prefer their volunteers to be at least 25 years old or to have strong experience in working with children, such as education or social work.

Trailblazer Foundation

www.thetrailblazerfoundation.org
Located .8 km south from Siem Reap city center, off Sivatha Road. Turn right at the Angkor Beer Distributor. Follow the zigzag in the road left and then right. Trailblazer is the first house on the left.
phone: 092 301 346

The foundation works with the poorest communities in Siem Reap province. Trailblazer is well-known for helping their partner villages secure clean and abundant water. They have helped over 50 villages. Accomplishments in 2016: constructed and distributed 468 water filters, drilled 124 wells, built 4 latrines with sanitation training, provided agricultural trainings to 100 people, built a secondary school, and distributed 100 bicycles to students.

How can I help? Office work, help construct water filters, work in the field, and work in the organic test gardens.

Useful Skills: communications, including writing, social media, graphic design, video production, podcasts, blogging. In-country fundraising, new project design, and program monitoring.

Volunteer Development Children's Association

www.vdca-cambodia.org/Volunteer-Program
Located in Tropeang Sess Village, Kork Chork Commune
See detailed directions on their website
phone: 092 271 208

VDCA welcomes both short (minimum one week) and long-term volunteers who have a real desire to make a difference in the lives of others and feel good about what they have to give.

How can I help? They employ a full-time staff of Khmer teachers and volunteers usually function as teaching assistants, under their supervision. You can teach English or other languages, hygiene, computer skills, support environmental education or assist other projects. They also place volunteers at their Free School in Siem Reap and at their rural projects in the dump area, 23km from town. Check out their website for their application and additional volunteer information and requirements.

Understanding Cambodia

Becoming a responsible traveler can start before you leave home. The key to being respectful in a foreign land is to be knowledgeable about that country's history, culture and customs. We will help you do your homework by providing stories, history, tips and useful information in the following chapters.

Brief History of Cambodia

The following summary will familiarize you with Cambodia's major historical events and governments during the last 1200 years, including Cambodia today. Although life is difficult for the majority of Cambodians, most express happiness that their country is currently at peace.

Ancient Kingdom of Angkor

The ancient Kingdom of Angkor spanned the years 802 AD to 1431 AD. At its peak, this powerful empire extended into Thailand, Vietnam and Laos and had a population of 30 million people. Many of the kings who ruled during this time associated themselves with one of the Hindu gods and built a temple to honor the god and himself. Most of the temples were built of stone and have myths and stories carved on their walls.

Today, ten thousand people a day, from all over the world, travel to Cambodia to visit these beautiful ancient temples, which comprise one of the largest religious structures in the world. The most famous temple is named Angkor Wat.

Early temples have carvings of Hindu gods and goddesses. One of Angkor's kings converted from Hinduism to Buddhism and started building temples with Buddhist images. The decline of the empire began in 1431 AD, when the Thai army invaded Cambodia. Cambodia lost a large part of its territory to Thailand and Vietnam, which still creates a feeling of resentment in some Cambodians today.

Even though the kingdom downsized, life for the peasants, who made up most of the population, did not change much over the next 500 years. They grew rice, lived simple lives in the rural areas and sought protection from those in power.

French Colonial Period

The French arrived in 1863 and turned Cambodia into a French colony by offering protection from Cambodia's invading neighbors, Vietnam and Thailand. They allowed King Norodom to be a symbolic king. The French started restoring Cambodia's ancient temples, which had been overgrown by jungle. In 1954, Cambodia gained independence from France. Prince Sihanouk then ruled the country until 1970. French influences can be found in the cuisine, in the colonial French architecture and in the long city parks.

US Bombing of Cambodia

In 1969 the Vietnam-American War spilled into Cambodia when the US started bombing neutral Cambodia. The US government believed Cambodia was helping the communists in Vietnam. International law states that it is illegal to bomb a neutral country, but the US bombing in Cambodia continued for four years. More bombs were dropped on Cambodia during that time than all the bombs dropped in WWII. In 1970, when Prince Sihanouk was on a trip to France, General Lon Nol took over Cambodia. Lon Nol supported the US in the Vietnam War. Between 1970 and 1975, several hundred thousand people died in Cambodia.

Khmer Rouge Genocide

The communist movement started in Cambodia in the 1940's to oppose the French rule. After independence from France, the communists, known as the Khmer Rouge, continued to work for better treatment of the peasant farmers in Cambodia.

In 1975, the Khmer Rouge, led by Pol Pot, took over Cambodia. They had a vision of creating a country without class, where everyone was equal at the level of a peasant farmer. To achieve this goal, they started executing people who were educated and middle or upper class. They forced everyone to move out of the cities and into slave labor camps in the rural areas. There was not enough food or medicine, so many people died from starvation or disease. During the Khmer Rouge's four-year reign of terror, at least 1.7 million people died.

The Khmer Rouge attacked Vietnam in an attempt to reclaim Cambodia's former territory during the Angkor Empire. This provoked Vietnam into invading Cambodia, ousting the Khmer Rouge and taking over the country in 1979. When the Vietnamese were fighting the Khmer Rouge, tens of thousands of Cambodians fled to the Thai border where they lived in refugee camps. Many emigrated to France, Australia and the United States.

Vietnamese-backed Government

Vietnam occupied and governed Cambodia from 1979 to 1991. The Vietnamese helped Cambodia rebuild roads, hospitals and schools that had been destroyed by the Khmer Rouge. Through the United Nations, the US initiated a world trade embargo against Cambodia in an attempt to bring down the communist government. As a result of the embargo, all humanitarian aid from the West was blocked for the 12 years following the genocide.

Civil War

In an effort to oust the Vietnamese-backed Cambodian government, several factions waged a civil war against the government including loyalists to the king, business interests. The largest group was the Khmer Rouge, still led by Pol Pot. The Khmer Rouge kept fighting the Cambodian government until 1998, when Pol Pot mysteriously died the day before he was to be extradited by the US.

Recent Governments

In 1991, the Vietnamese left Cambodia following the collapse of the Soviet Union and Vietnam's subsequent loss of aid from the USSR. The United Nations took over and helped Cambodians prepare for democratic elections, which were held in 1993. Prince Ranariddh won the election, but Hun Sen, the former prime minister, would not agree to step down, so they formed a coalition government and were named co-prime ministers. Hun Sen subsequently won the national elections in 1998, 2003 and 2008.

Cambodia Today

Cambodian culture is still strongly influenced by the Angkor Period. Music and classical royal dance from the ancient empire are still performed today. There are remnants of French influence in the form of colonial architecture, parks and food.

Cambodia is currently one of the poorest countries in the world. It is still recovering from the Khmer Rouge genocide, when a quarter of the population, including most of the educated people (such as doctors and teachers) were killed. There still is a shortage of schools and hospitals.

Thirty percent of the population does not have access to clean drinking water. Nearly half of the children in Cambodia are malnourished. There are 4 to 6 million landmines in Cambodian soil and, on the average, two people a week are injured.

Government concessions of land and community forests to private companies for development have fueled illegal logging, evictions and loss of livelihoods for rural residents. Now many rural people seek work in neighboring countries, but are commonly exploited while there.

Prime Minister Hun Sen has held power since 1985. He is known for persecuting his opponents. Human rights violations are common. Recurring protests in support of higher wages, land rights or greater political freedom have been brutally dealt with by military police who sometimes kill the protesters.

Cambodia is a beautiful country with a rich cultural heritage. Its greatest challenges today are poverty, recovering from the wounds of war and genocide, and government corruption.

Speaking a Few Words of Khmer

Greet adults with your hands held together in prayer-style in front of your face. And say: **Jum Reep Sur**

For a more informal hello which is like saying "doing OK?" say: **Sok Sa Bai?**

And if you want to answer that question, say the same thing without a question tone: **Sok Sa Bai**

To say thank you: **Aw Koon**

To ask the driver to stop say: **Chop Chop**

To tell the kids trying to sell you stuff "no thank you": **Aw Tay**

Lieng, a Genocide Survivor's Story

Cambodia's relatively recent genocide has left scars that still affect the entire country and population. It is difficult for most of us to fathom this trauma until we read the details as told by a survivor. This excerpt is from the book *Soul Survivors* by Bhavia C. Wagner. Her book gives voice to women and children who survived the Khmer Rouge's secret genocide and the two decades of civil war that followed. This moving personal narrative documents the life of Lieng, one of 50 medical doctors who survived the genocide, when nearly two million people died between 1975 and 1979 from execution, starvation, or disease. Here, Lieng tells her story.

April 17, 1975 is stamped in my mind because our lives were changed forever from that day on. I could have left Cambodia before 1975, but didn't consider it because I had no idea the Khmer Rouge would be so cruel. My father used to say that even if Cambodia became communist, it would be alright because communists believe in equality.

I was in my fifth year of medical school at the time. My father was a surgeon and he wanted one of his children to become a doctor. I agreed, because practicing medicine is a service. I could have gone to school in France where three of my six brothers and sisters lived, but my father thought it would be better if I studied medicine in Cambodia where the education was more practical. There were about fifty students in my class and I was one of five women. My husband, Toek, was also in medical school. We had a five-year-old daughter, Chhada and our son Noravin was two.

At first we were very happy when the Khmer Rouge took over Cambodia because we thought the war was over. They marched into Phnom Penh like a parade and we congratulated them, clapping our hands and yelling "Bravo! We want peace." We were shocked when the soldiers turned and pointed their guns at us and ordered us to leave our homes. They said it would only be for three days, but if we didn't cooperate, we would be shot.

My husband became very anxious when he saw the Khmer Rouge shoot a Lon Nol soldier on the street. He urged us to hurry up and leave. I nervously held my two young children as my father, still dressed in his white doctor's uniform, packed a small box of medical instruments and my mother gathered jewelry, gold and clothes to take with us.

The Khmer Rouge came to the door and forced us to leave immediately, so we weren't able to go upstairs to get the rest of our things. My family had three cars and we wanted to take one for my pregnant sister, but we couldn't because there were 100,000 people in the street, so we walked. We watched in horror as the Khmer Rouge killed former Lon Nol soldiers and civilians who didn't follow orders. Blood filled the streets.

We planned to meet up with my in-laws and travel with them, so when we reached their street, my parents, daughter and three sisters stepped off the main road. Instantly, a soldier pointed his gun at them and ordered them to lie down on the ground. The crowd pushed me, my husband and our son forward and, to my alarm, our family became separated. I cried a lot, but knew we had no choice. We could have died if we tried to follow them. Only an angel could have helped us then.

We walked southeast, by way of Highway 1. The Khmer Rouge didn't allow us to stop and rest until dark. We had left home with practically nothing and had to share the few clothes my youngest sister had packed for us. I bought pork for dinner. I didn't realize it would be the last time I would spend money in four years.

We traveled for a week, forced ahead by the Khmer Rouge, until we were near the Vietnamese border in Kandal Province. The air was full of smoke from a burning temple and I saw the swollen rotting bodies of dead Lon Nol soldiers. I heard a husband and wife quarreling and when the fact that he was a former Lon Nol soldier slipped out, the Khmer Rouge came over, took him away and shot him.

We were ordered to move in with a farming couple, into their wooden stilt house. They didn't trust us "new people." Every two or three days the Khmer Rouge gave each

person a small can of rice and a little salt. It wasn't enough, so we ate fish and clams that we caught in the river. Then, the Khmer Rouge took away my small radio, which distressed me because I lost touch with the outside world.

We stayed in Kandal Province for two months. Every day I watched and waited for my parents and my daughter as I worked, caring for young children while my husband labored in rice fields. One day, the Khmer Rouge announced that we could move to our native villages. My husband decided we should go to Kompot Province in hope of finding my parents and daughter.

The Khmer Rouge took us south, by boat. The first night we slept in a temple and then our group of 100 traveling people walked across Takeo Province. It took us all day to cross a stretch of land where nothing was growing, not even grass. We needed fuel to cook our rice, so my husband broke up the wooden shoes that were given to him when he was cutting thorn trees.

The journey to Kompot Province took two months. It was exhausting and on the way my husband became very sick with malaria. First, I traded gold for medicine. Then the local people told me that sdav tree leaves would bring down his fever, so I prepared a medicinal tea, which proved to be effective.

After crossing the Neareay Mountains, we finally arrived at our native village of Trapeng Thom. We were disappointed to learn that my parents and daughter were not there, but we were glad to find my husband's parents and my cousin Sophine. We asked the Khmer Rouge leader if we could live with my in-laws. He allowed us to stay only two days and then sent us to live in Trapeng Cheutiel Village about eight kilometers away. We became very sad when we learned that the Khmer Rouge had killed my newly married brother-in-law, just because he wore glasses. The Khmer Rouge thought people with glasses were educated and should be purged from Cambodian society.

For four years I lived like a slave. At first I told the truth about being a doctor, but people warned me to hide my identity, lest I be killed, so then I said I was a hospital worker. Many of the local farmers, the "old people," scorned me because I didn't know how to winnow rice. I couldn't work very hard, being still weak from the miscarriage I had shortly before we were evacuated from Phnom Penh. I also had a bad knee and couldn't walk very well. I was grateful to an older woman who treated me with sour herbs and stopped my knee pain. At first, my job was to dig out tree stumps, which was very difficult work. Later, I was assigned the miserable task of making compost from human feces.

A few months later, my husband was sent far away to do heavy work, while I worked close to home, watching children and planting rice. The water in the rice paddy was chest-high and full of scaly green leeches. I hated the leeches, which were as big as three fingers and I tied the bottom of my pants in several places to try to keep them out.

Not long after my husband left, the Khmer Rouge ordered me to live near the weaving center, which was the central meeting place.

When I asked why, they told me that they wanted to observe me because I was one of the "educated people." I had to be very careful about what I said. They watched everything I did, even boiling water. I hid two syringes and a little gold in a coconut tree near my new house, but I was afraid the Khmer Rouge would find them, so I put them in the hem of my blouse. Then they watched me bathe, so I buried my valuables. One day the Khmer Rouge told me to move back to Trapeng Cheutiel Village and I was disappointed when I couldn't retrieve the gold and the syringes.

In 1976, there were twenty families living in my village. One by one they were killed. I had just delivered the baby of a former Lon Nol soldier, when the Khmer Rouge took the whole family away to be killed. One day, when I was harvesting rice, the Khmer Rouge came and I watched them tie the hands of two women behind their backs and march them away to be executed. Next, an ethnic Vietnamese woman and her entire family were murdered. I felt sick when I saw the legs and hands of a dead ethnic Chinese girl sticking out of the ground after a dog dug up her grave. By 1977, only four families in our village were left. Terrified that we would be the next to die, we focused solely on our work and never spoke to each other.

In February of 1977, the Khmer Rouge took my husband away, I don't know why. He had been building a dike and the small shovel he was using had broken. Maybe that was the reason. The Khmer Rouge tied his hands behind his back and made him walk in front of them. He passed by the field where I was harvesting rice and I ran toward him. "Do you want to die," the old people called after me. I remembered my son and I knew I had to turn back. My spirit was not in my body, but I felt responsible for my young child. I felt helpless and very sad because I had already lost my parents and my daughter. Now my husband was gone. I walked around unconsciously, on automatic, feeling like I was living without my soul. After my husband was taken away, I was afraid the Khmer Rouge would come for me. No one wanted to be seen speaking to me.

I survived the Khmer Rouge by working hard, keeping my identity a secret and not talking too much. When I helped deliver a baby, the family usually gave me some food. I think being nice to my neighbors, being flexible and not arguing also helped, which was easy for me, because I have a gentle nature. A man asked me to marry him after my husband was taken away, but I refused and said I was too old. The local people said, "No, you are like guava fruit, better with age," but I still declined.

The Khmer Rouge ordered me to move near the mountain, where my sister-in-law lived. I had to build my own house from bamboo and thatch. I worked in very cold, chest-deep water, pulling out rice seedlings for replanting, until nine or ten at night. The weather was cold and I didn't have a blanket for sleeping, but fortunately it was harvest time and our soup was thick with rice. Usually, the Khmer Rouge gave ten people only one small can of rice each day.

When I got my rice ration, I ate some, then put the rest in a coconut shell and took it back to my young son. One afternoon, a woman told me that the Khmer Rouge had seen me do that. I didn't care because I wanted my son to survive and I was worried about his nutrition. He was hungry and often ate tree bark and tiny frogs. I planted sweet potatoes for the Khmer Rouge, but I didn't have the right to eat them and instead I ate banana tree trunks and papaya tree roots. During the dry season I used a mosquito net to catch small fish and during the rainy season I gathered dead fish, salted them, stored them in the roof thatch and later made them into fish paste for my son.

I became worried when my son turned very pale and anemic. I took my sick little boy to the "hospital," which was in a former school. I had to go there because the Khmer Rouge wouldn't let me care for him at home and miss work. When we arrived, they assigned my son a bed and the "nurse," a twelve-year-old girl wearing black Khmer Rouge clothes, came over and asked what illness he had. She just inquired, but then gave the same medicine for everything. The Khmer Rouge used traditional medicine, tablets of different colors. They also had serum for injections, sweet and salty water stored in soft drink bottles covered with plastic bags. That water frightened me as did their injections of coconut milk. Fortunately, my son improved and three weeks later, we returned home.

My cousin Sophine became sick, so I took her to the district hospital, where they had better medicine. The hospital was in a temple and as we arrived I saw seriously ill patients being carried there in hammocks, since the Khmer Rouge would not allow ox carts to be used for transporting sick people. The Khmer Rouge never used anesthetics for small operations, so the screams of patients filled the building. I didn't watch because I feared I might be accused of being too inquisitive. I recognized a man working there who was a trained medical assistant. Later I heard that he was killed by the Khmer Rouge.

In January 1979, we were relieved to hear that the Vietnamese had taken over Phnom Penh. If I had a husband or man to direct my life then maybe I could have escaped from the Khmer Rouge at that time, but I was passive and was forced to go with them through the forests of Kompong Speu and Pursat Provinces as they fled from the Vietnamese. My five-year-old son and my cousin Sophine were with me.

The weather was extreme, too hot to travel during the mid-day and cold and damp at night. I became sick with a high fever. My head was burning and I thought I might die. A woman and her family gave me a very bitter tea made from the nim tree and took care of me until I recovered.

We had to cross Sam Sep Chuan (Mountain of Thirty Levels). Small children, old people, horses, cows and anyone who couldn't climb the steep mountain were left behind to die. We started before sunrise and walked for forty-two hours without food or water. On the second day, I cut a vine to get some liquid for my son. We arrived at midnight, totally exhausted, at a place with murky water that we used to cook rice. The next day, we walked past Oral Mountain where the smell from dead soldiers was horrendous.

We lived in Pursat Province with the Khmer Rouge for one miserable month. They let us

bathe only once a week. One day, the Khmer Rouge ordered the people of Bak Kan Seng Village to dig a pond. When they finished, the Khmer Rouge massacred them and pushed them into the hole they had dug. So when the Khmer Rouge told us to dig a small pond, I felt weak from terror because I knew we would be killed the next day. By a stroke of luck, we were saved the next morning when some people passed by and invited us to escape with them. It was March of 1979 and I walked home with my son and my cousin Sophine, through Kompong Chanang Province toward Phnom Penh. It was a difficult journey. At one point we ran across a stream to escape being killed by the Khmer Rouge.

As soon as I arrived in Phnom Penh, I went directly to my old house hoping to find my relatives, but no one was there. I walked through the empty house and saw that most things were just as we left them, four years before. Our books on Buddhism were still on the shelf along with my husband's class notes and my father's dissertation. A Vietnamese soldier came in and told me that no one was permitted to live in that area. As I was leaving, I stopped and wrote a message to my family on the front gate saying that I had come looking for them. Then I walked over to the medical clinic my parents had struggled to build and saw that the new government had taken over the building.

A couple of days later I ran into Sovan, my cousin and friend from high school and she invited us to come live with her. Every morning I went out begging for food. When some kind people gave me two or three cans of rice, I pounded it into a powder and fried it with banana to make *chek chean*, which I then traded for more rice.

I wandered around the city, alone and barefoot, collecting basic household items. There were plenty of goods available and if I had been more ambitious I could have become rich, but I didn't want to take more than I needed. I saw buildings filled with lamps, radios and televisions. Later, I heard that they were taken to Vietnam.

I gradually found out what happened to my family. A man who escaped from the Khmer Rouge at the end of 1978 told me that my husband had been put in prison, in a cave in Chrous Mlou mountain and when the Vietnamese came, the Khmer Rouge threw hand-grenades into the prison and killed everyone.

I learned from a cousin that my mother became sick and died along Highway 1 only three months after she left Phnom Penh. My sixty-year-old father worked in Kompot Province, tending cows and making rope until 1977, when he became sick and was taken to a hospital. They gave him an injection that killed him and he was thrown into a mass grave with other corpses. I also heard that my daughter was dead.

My three sisters who left Phnom Penh with my parents all died. Uthiucharey was pregnant and gave birth along Highway 1. The baby died shortly after delivery and then Uthiucharey died. Her husband, a university history professor, was in Australia at that time. Pol Pot had invited the intellectuals who were living abroad to return and then

killed them. Uthiucharey's husband came back to Cambodia in 1977 and we assume he was murdered because no one has ever heard from him.

My second sister, Kola Watano, was so upset after her husband was killed by the Khmer Rouge that she went insane for a while and later she and her daughter died. My youngest sister, Panha Theariny, was taken away by the Khmer Rouge and murdered for no reason. I was the only surviving member of my family in Cambodia in 1979.

Not long after I arrived in Phnom Penh I met Dr. Khun Nget, one of my father's former students. He asked me to work in a clinic next to Tek Tla temple. For the first time in four years, my son and I had enough rice to eat. Later, a friend from medical school advised me to apply for a job with the Ministry of Health. I was assigned to work at April 17 Hospital. I don't know why they chose that name for a hospital, because it is so full of pain. It is the day the murderous Khmer Rouge regime began.

The hospital was filthy and the first thing I did was clean it thoroughly, with help from the other medical staff. We didn't have enough medical supplies, equipment, medicine, or staff, but did what we could. I went out and bought plaster for making casts and we collected medical supplies from other hospitals. I worked on the third floor in general medicine, with only one other doctor, mainly caring for malnourished patients who were very skinny and had big swollen bellies. There were only two doctors in the hospital that had expertise and they came over from Vietnam.

After the Khmer Rouge regime there were only forty doctors left in the country. Nearly all the older doctors had died, so we had no specialists or experts. There wasn't a single psychiatrist in Cambodia. Only eighteen out of the fifty medical students in my class survived and I was the only woman. I still had two of the seven years of medical school left, but the last year is practice. I went back to medical school and graduated in nine months because Cambodia desperately needed doctors.

After receiving my medical degree, I became director of a hospital's emergency and recovery rooms. Some of my colleagues worked in Cambodia a while and then went to live abroad because the conditions here were so terrible. Hang Nor was one of the survivors from my medical class. He worked in a refugee camp in Thailand and later was the lead actor in the film The Killing Fields.

At the end of 1979, I asked a French TV reporter who was visiting the hospital if he could help me find my relatives in France, so he took a picture of me and sent it to France. I was overjoyed when my relatives wrote me. When the hospital director found out what I had done, he sent me away to study communist policy and eat only corn for a month with sixty other people at a re-education center in Phnom Penh run by the Vietnamese. After that experience, I was careful about speaking to foreigners.

In 1980, a relative bicycled 150 kilometers to bring my daughter Chhada to me from Kompot Province. I could hardly believe it was Chhada. I thought she had died. I didn't recognize her until I studied her face and saw that it resembled her father's. I felt sorry for her, but I held back my tears because I thought I needed to be brave.

Lieng, a Genocide Survivor's Story

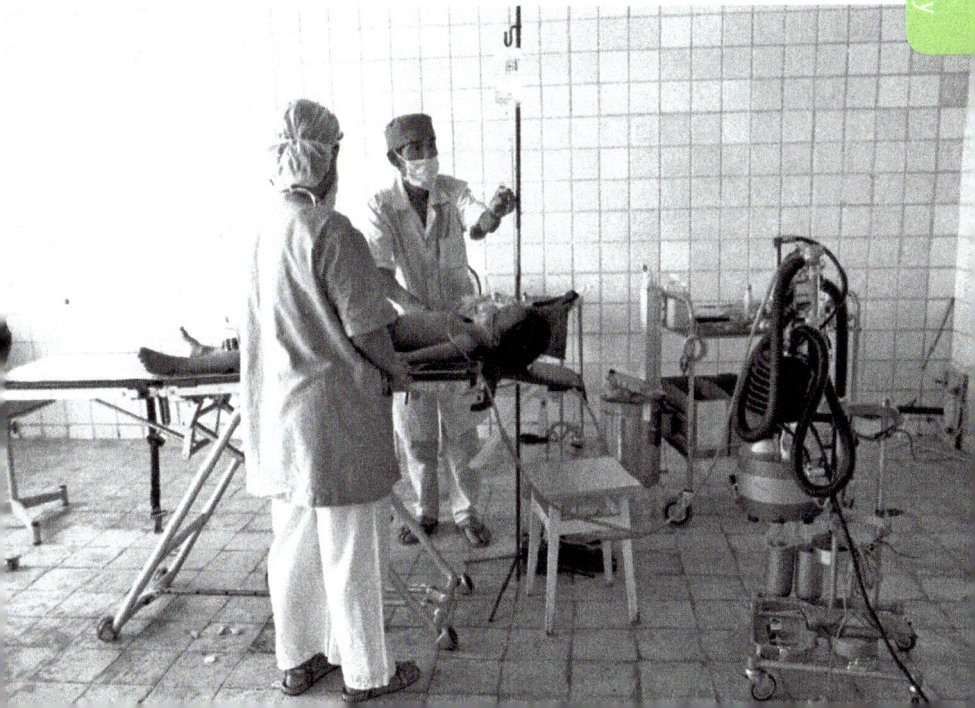

I wanted to have a normal mother-daughter relationship with Chhada, but we were not close like mothers and daughters who stayed together. I felt a barrier between us that blocked her love for me. When Chhada was young I knew she was very intelligent, but after the Khmer Rouge regime she never did well in school and didn't want to continue her education after completing high school. The Khmer Rouge made her carry heavy loads on her head and I saw the scars on her scalp. She was very different from her brother, who lived with me during the Khmer Rouge regime.

I saw a picture of Pol Pot for the first time when I hosted a French delegation at the hospital and accompanied them to Toul Sleng museum, the former Khmer Rouge interrogation and torture center. I stood there in disbelief when I realized that Pol Pot had been my French teacher in 1961 at Chareoun Vichea High School, when his name was Saloth Sar. I was shocked! I imagined how terrible his mother must have felt to have had such a child.

I just don't understand why Pol Pot ordered Cambodians to kill their own people. I didn't know him well, but I remember he was a very serious person. Later, I discovered that the wife of Ieng Sary was my Khmer literature teacher at Norodom High School. Pol Pot, Ieng Sary and Khieu Samphan were the three top leaders of the Khmer Rouge in 1975 and still were twenty years later and I knew all of them.

At the beginning of 1981, I was elected leader of the Hospital Trade Union, organized under the authority of the Communist Party.

Besides working at the hospital, I also taught physiology at the University of Phnom Penh Medical School. In 1982, I went to Hanoi to study emergency room procedures, because at that time Vietnam was the only place we could get a scholarship. In 1983, East German doctors came to work with us and we watched, slightly amused, as they quarreled with the Vietnamese doctors over technical points.

Under socialism we were trained to work hard and set a good example for the next generation. I worked at the public hospital six days a week, seven hours a day. The government paid doctors only $20 per month, so I needed to have a private practice at home, to earn extra income. In 1984, I was so exhausted I collapsed on the floor with bak kamlang (broken strength). I was sent on a month-long holiday in Russia on the Black Sea with twenty other people, but it wasn't very relaxing because I was one of the leaders.

Comparing 1980 with 1990, I can see that our living conditions improved under the new communist government, but there were also shortcomings. Some Vietnamese came to cooperate, but others wanted to dominate us and control our thinking. Cambodia was only open to the USSR and other communist countries. No one was permitted to study French or English, only Vietnamese was allowed. The high school curriculum didn't include history, because they didn't want anyone to know about other cultures or think of improvements. When the Khmer Rouge regime ended, everyone was equal, barefoot and bare-handed, but now many high-ranking government leaders own several houses.

I see many problems in Cambodia today. Government corruption makes the average person worse off. The education system is not good. Students attend school only half a day because there is a lack of teachers, so they don't learn a full curriculum. Nearly half of the older women in Cambodia have health problems related to the Khmer Rouge period and as a medical doctor I see a lot of nervous disorders and circulation problems in women. When something triggers a woman's memory, like seeing a person's face who reminds her of her dead husband, it is common for her to have a seizure. I've also seen a lot of insane women on the streets of Phnom Penh. My aunt lost her sanity after the Khmer Rouge killed her husband and children; now she doesn't make sense when she speaks. I thank God I am still sane.

In 1992, I passed the entrance exam to get a postgraduate degree in anesthesiology and went through a three-year program with nine other doctors, studying under a visiting French expert at the University of Phnom Penh. It was more difficult to remember the lessons because I am older. I finished school at age fifty, which is retirement age, but I agreed to work and teach in the medical school for six years.

I had good parents and I appreciate how they supported me and encouraged me to go to the university. When I started medical school I just wanted to get a degree and afterward I planned to stay home and take care of my children. Now I'm glad I have a degree because I see that widows who didn't have careers prior to 1975 met more difficulty as they tried to earn money to support their children.

When I reflect on my life, I see that it has not been a happy one. As a widow, I had to make all the decisions without having anyone to discuss them with. I miss feeling my husband's love for me. I worried about my children and was afraid I could not provide a good future for them. I did the best I could to be a good mother, to teach my children about Cambodian culture and how to be good citizens.

I don't worry as much as I used to. I feel satisfied that I chose a good husband for my daughter Chhada. He is kind and likes his work as a doctor. Chhada sells medicine at my home clinic and cares for her little boy. My son Noravin is studying at the Institute of Agriculture and he will get a job when he graduates. I just continue to work hard and am patient, because to be human is to always have problems, big or small. People see that I am strong and solid, like a stone, but my heart is very soft.

Cambodian Holidays and Culture

Understanding local customs will not only enhance your travel experience, but it will give you the cultural sensitivity to act respectfully. Cambodians are very gracious and they welcome tourists to join the festivities of the Cambodian holidays. The three most significant holidays are the Cambodian New Year in mid-April, Ancestors Remembrance Day in late September and the Water Festival in early November.

A suggestion for culturally appropriate behavior is to carefully observe the Cambodians. Notice when they take off their shoes, how modestly they dress, how they greet each other, how they sit, how they do or don't touch each other, how they serve and eat their food and their tone of voice. They will think highly of you if you follow their example. The following descriptions are a contribution from the Cornell University Southeast Asia Program.

New Year

The Cambodian New Year takes place in mid-April, during the dry season when farmers are not busy working in the fields. Astrologers determine the time and date by calculating the exact moment the new animal protector (tiger, dragon, or snake, etc. – from the Chinese zodiac) arrives. Cambodians spend the entire month in preparation for the celebration, cleaning and decorating their house with candles, lights, star-shaped lanterns and flowers. During the first three days of the New Year, everyone travels to the Buddhist temples to offer food to the monks.

Pchum Ben

Ancestors Remembrance Day or Pchum Ben is a religious ceremony in September when Cambodians remember the spirits of their dead relatives. For fifteen days, people in Cambodian villages take turns bringing food to the temples. On the fifteenth and final day, everyone dresses in their finest clothing and travels together to the temple. Families bring overflowing baskets of flowers and children offer food and presents to the monks. Everyone says prayers to help their ancestors pass on to a better life. According to Khmer belief, those who do not follow the practices of Pchum Ben are cursed by their angry ancestors.

Water Festival

Another very colorful festival is the Water Festival or the Festival of the Reversing Current. It takes place in late October or early November and marks the reversal of the Tonle Sap River, so that it once again flows south from the Tonle Sap Lake into the Mekong River.

The highlight of the three-day festival is the boat race that is held in Phnom Penh.

Individual villages build their own boats by hollowing out a log to make a dugout canoe that is rowed by as many as forty people! The prow and the stern of the canoe turn upward and the prow is painted with an eye, just like the war vessels on the wall of the temples at Angkor Thom.

On the first two days of the festival, pairs of boats race each other. At sunset on the third day, there is a big race and everyone believes that if the river is happy, the fish will be plentiful and the rice crop will flourish.

Weddings

Weddings are the most important social events in the lives of young people. Men usually get married between the ages of 19 and 24 and women between the ages of 16 and 22.

Most marriages are arranged by the parents. The bride and groom meet for the first time shortly before their wedding. There are traditional ways in which a family should decide if a partner is suitable or not. Each family appoints a representative to investigate the other family, who makes sure that they are honest and, hopefully, wealthy. Once the two families agree to the wedding, they exchange gifts of plants and food and then they consult an astrologer, who chooses a lucky date for the ceremony.

The wedding ceremony takes place at the bride's house. The bride and groom exchange gifts and rings. Their wrists are tied together with red thread that has been soaked in holy water. A Buddhist monk gives a talk and married guests pass around a candle to bless the new couple. After the ceremony, there is a grand feast. People eat fruit, meat and small round cakes filled with rice or coconut. Musicians play traditional instruments.

Funerals

Most Cambodians are Buddhists. Accordingly, they do not look on death as the end of life. Rather, they consider it the beginning of a new life that they hope will be better than the one which ended. Therefore, just as performing the wedding rituals correctly is very important, it is also very important to perform the ceremonies for death in the correct Buddhist tradition. Otherwise, the relative will not be able to pass on to their new life.

When a person dies, the body is washed, dressed and put into a coffin. Flowers and a photograph of the deceased are usually put on top of the coffin, which is then carried to a special Buddhist temple to be cremated. All the family members walk with the coffin to the temple. If the deceased person was important in the community, everyone in the village joins the procession. Family members sometimes show their sorrow by wearing white clothing and shaving their heads.

Because the rituals connected to death affect the ability of the dead person to have a happy next life, many Cambodians are still distraught because they were not able to perform the correct rituals for loved ones who died under the Khmer Rouge regime.

Birthdays

Cambodian children do not celebrate their birthdays and it is not a special day for them. Often their parents just remember what season they were born in, but not the exact day. During the Khmer Rouge years, many people were separated from their families and they lost their birth certificates. However, all Cambodians know which year they were born and what it means according to the Chinese animal calendar.

Language

Cambodia's national language is Khmer. It is the language taught in the country's schools and is used in government documents. The Khmer writing system comes from an Indian alphabet that was brought into Cambodia over a thousand years ago. In Khmer, everyone refers to each other as older brother and older sister, or Aunt and Uncle. Many ancient words are borrowed from Pali or Sanskrit and many more words that are recent are from French, words such as "chocolate" and "gateaux." Khmer grammar is very simple. For example, there are no tenses. If you want to change "I go to the market" into the past tense, you just add the word "already".

Khmer is precise in ways that English is not. Like many languages, it has many words for articles that are useful for Cambodian people. For example, there are over one hundred words for rice! In addition, there are different words for "you," depending on whether you are speaking to a child, a parent, a Buddhist monk, or a member of the royal family.

Under the Khmer Rouge regime, they tried to forbid some of these pronouns so that everyone was placed on the same level. Among educated Cambodians over sixty years of age, French is still a second language. In the mid 1980s, however, French was overtaken informally by English as the European language that urban Cambodians wanted to learn. In rural areas, not many people speak a foreign language.

Literature

The greatest piece of literature in Khmer is called *The Reamker*. It is the Cambodian adaptation of the Indian epic of the Ramayana. It dates from the fifteenth or sixteenth century. The story of Hanuman and Sovann Macha is derived from this story and made into a dance. Many Cambodian dances and shadow puppet plays are also taken from the Cambodian version of The Ramayana. The Ramayana is found in many cultures throughout Southeast Asia.

Cambodians also like to tell their children chbaps or moral proverbs, which school children memorize, as well as stories from the Reamker of folk tales. The chbap teaches the values of Cambodian society, such as being obedient to your elders and protecting those who are less fortunate than you are. Here are some examples of Cambodian proverbs: "Don't take the straight path or the winding path. Take the path your ancestors have taken." "Don't let an angry man wash dishes; don't let a hungry man guard rice."

Cambodian Food *by Kathie Carpenter*

In a traditional Cambodian meal every bite refreshes the palate. Cambodians enjoy foods with vibrant flavors - sweet, sour, salty and bitter - but instead of contrasting seasonings within a single dish, the whole meal is a palette of separate dishes, each emphasizing a different taste and texture. Each diner creates their own culinary composition by balancing and contrasting bites in unique and personalized compositions, depending on their taste and mood.

Textures also contrast and refresh. Playful alternations of creamy and crunchy prevent dulling of the senses and raw alternates with cooked to continually reawaken the taste buds and the taster. Cambodian cooks serve pungent wild gathered vegetables (don't call them weeds!) alongside familiar cultivated ones and old favorites can appear in surprising guises - banana blossoms are often eaten long before the fruits appear, mango and watermelon can be used green and unripe and pineapple is often used as a vegetable, stir fried or in soups. Soup is eaten with the meal as a palate cleanser between bites, rather than as a separate course.

Cambodian cuisine is distinctively and deliciously its own. Cambodia is historically the heartland of an empire that stretched over a million square kilometers across mainland Southeast Asia, so it is not surprising that Cambodian foodways have influenced Thai, Lao and Vietnamese cooking, even as it has been influenced by them, as well as by the cooking of China, India and France.

The traditional Cambodian diet is very healthy. It contains very little fat, but the bright tastes of kaffir limes, lemongrass, ginger and tamarind are complemented by the richer, fuller undernotes of roasted garlic, black pepper and prahok, a quintessentially Cambodian seasoning made from salted, fermented fish. Aromatic seasonings, many even lacking names in English, are blended together in a paste called kroueng, used as a curry base, marinade, rub or soup stock. Kroueng gives Cambodian food a spiciness and aroma that can wake up the most jaded palate, even though traditional Cambodian food is not at all hot and chilies are used sparingly and usually only on the side.

> **Etiquette Tip:** *When eating with Cambodians, don't heap your plate with food; instead, take just a couple of spoonfuls out of the serving bowl and eat that before getting another small serving.*

Cambodian Food

Even cooking and serving containers impart distinctive tastes to this complex and subtle cuisine - some dishes derive their signature taste from a steaming in banana leaves, while others take on the aroma of the clay pots they are simmered in.

The Cambodian diet is sustainably linked to the climate and environment of Cambodia. It is local, seasonal and fresh, fresh, fresh! In the rainy season, monsoon flooding can bring over half the landmass under water, so it is natural that fish and rice are the main staple foods. While travelers' tales often sensationalize close encounters with ingredients like spiders, crocodiles, lizards, or silkworm larvae, please bear in mind that Cambodian foodways are intimately linked with the contours of the land and the cycles of the seasons and the waterways. Little is wasted, distinctive tastes are treasured and wild food-gathering expeditions are joyful occasions enjoyed by the whole family. An

element of sustainability comes from the fact that wild foods and garnishes can be gathered as needed and enjoyed at their freshest and even in urban markets, you will see piles of wild foods that continue to be savored by residents of Cambodia's largest cities. When seasonal bounty is preserved, the flavor is concentrated and enhanced by

pickling, salting and drying, which all add prized dimensions of pungency.

Food in Cambodia is only enjoyed if it is shared. If you are fortunate enough to be invited to a meal in a Cambodian family home, expect all diners to share several dishes and to serve themselves from the communal pot. However, even in a restaurant, keeping your own entree to yourself looks downright antisocial and it will dull your palate to eat repeated bites of the same thing. To appreciate the liveliness of traditional Cambodian cooking, order several foods that contrast in flavor and texture and experiment with as many orders and combinations as you can imagine.

Below are some dishes you will want to try, presented together as an example of a menu that offers contrasts of rich and creamy, fresh and crunchy, sour and refreshing, juicy and fragrant, pungent and bitter. But don't be afraid to be adventurous!

A possible menu providing plenty of contrasts and featuring some of Cambodia's most beloved dishes might include:

Amok curried fish steamed in banana leaves with coconut cream and kaffir lime leaves (delicious tofu amok is also available)

Nyoum trayong chaek crunchy banana blossom salad with fresh herbs

Samlor machu trey tamarind pineapple fish soup

Kari sach moan red chicken curry

Pomelo salad with peanuts

Chruch rum sat dong kchai ang grilled pork fillet stuffed with young coconut

Eating Spiders

Want to provide comic relief for your traveling companions? Visit Romdeng and ask for the grilled spider dish. I haven't yet tried this myself, but I'm gearing up for it for my upcoming trip. I've been telling myself, "It's just a crab that lives on the land," so I think I'm about ready to add arachnids to the list of foods I've tried in different countries.

If spider isn't your thing, there are other terrific dishes to enjoy, sometimes with the added bonus of watching someone who's not you having a new culinary experience.

Shoshana Kerewsky

Sex Tourism

Sex tourism is at a crisis level in Cambodia and is the polar opposite of responsible tourism. Sex tourism violates the human rights of women and children. UNICEF estimates that there are over 5000 child prostitutes under the age of 16 in Phnom Penh. Male tourists who think they are "dating" or "having a good time" with the Khmer girls they meet in the bar or karaoke club are, in reality, exploiting and abusing girls who grew up in poverty and became victims of the sex industry.

We believe sex tourism is one of the greatest tragedies of our times. This soul-shattering abuse of women and children comes in many forms. For example, a male teacher in the United States made frequent trips to Cambodia and took school supplies with him. Upon returning from Cambodia, he was arrested at the airport by United States government officials for luring children into his hotel room and sexually abusing them.

When you visit Cambodia, you will see young and old men tourists hanging out with young Cambodian girls, especially in hotels and bars. Sex tourism in Southeast Asia is promoted on the internet and through guidebooks. Some sex tourists take girls as "escorts" for their travels. You may see them in restaurants and on the plane. Others pick up girls in the bars and bring them back to their hotel.

"What's the problem?" some people ask. The problem is that the girl is not in school, she is being used like a piece of property, she is at risk for sexually transmitted diseases including AIDS and, from the traditional Cambodian viewpoint and often the girl's opinion, her life is ruined. No one will want to marry her. Girls in Cambodia are usually protected by their families. They do not date boys and their parents arrange their marriages with their consent.

Thousands of girls in Cambodia are sold into prostitution. How does this happen? Traffickers prey on poor rural families. They tell a mother that they have a housekeeping job in the city for her daughter. The trafficker offers the mother the girl's first month's wages. Normally, this mother would protect her daughter, but because she is so desperately poor and the family may not even have enough food to eat, she agrees. Then the trafficker takes the girl to the city and sells her to a brothel where she is usually drugged, raped, maybe even shocked with electric cattle prods and forced to serve customers. She is held in the brothel for years, until she has "worked off her debt," which is the fee the brothel owner paid the trafficker. It is cruel slavery.

As responsible tourists, you can boycott establishments that allow sex tourism. You can ask the hotel about their policy on sex tourism when booking your room. Consumer pressure will encourage hotel owners to stop looking away and instead take a stand to protect the human rights of women and children.

If you see a situation where a child is being abused, you can report it to the ChildSafe Hotline 012-311-112.

How hotels prevent sex tourism and pedophiles

Socially responsible hotels require all guests to present identification papers. The sexually-exploited do not have ID. Here is an example of a policy:

Visitors policy: *To preserve the security and tranquility of all our guests - and in compliance with Cambodian law, only guests who have their identification papers (valid passport / valid Khmer ID) registered by our reception may enter rooms. All guests have to be registered at check in. No unregistered individual is allowed in any room at any time.*

Children less than 16 years: *must be accompanied by adult relative / legal guardians with documents proving they are family member (passport) / legal custodian (proof of adoption or guardianship).*

Aid Organizations: Helpful or Corrupt?

Forty percent of the children in Cambodia are malnourished. One third of the population lacks clean drinking water. Many innocent girls are sex-trafficked. Every week two people step on landmines. There are thousands of children living and working in the streets.

Where does one begin to help? And how do you know your money is going to do any good at all, especially when we all know there are corrupt aid organizations? Here are some guidelines.

Most Helpful Aid Organizations

- Work with the poorest of the poor and people in crisis – landmine survivors, families with AIDS, trafficked girls, street children, or people living in extreme poverty. Help them rebuild their self-confidence and ability to transform their lives.

- Create self-sufficiency by empowering people and communities to help themselves – through credit programs, vocational training, savings programs, or education.

- Encourage local initiatives and coopera-tion. Ask "What do you dream of and what do you need to achieve your goal?" Provide matching incentive grants.

- Employ Cambodian staff.

Moderately Helpful Aid Organizations

Foreigners tell Cambodians what they need and do everything for them. Although the program may provide needed help, this approach creates a sense of helplessness and dependency on foreigners to solve their problems. In the long-run, it is better to support a Cambodian student through medical school than send a team of foreign doctors for two weeks. Or why not do both?

Corrupt Aid Organizations

Director pockets all or part of the money donated for the humanitarian project. May use disabled people or orphans to elicit sympathy and donations from tourists. This is a common occurrence and sometimes difficult to detect.

Suggestion

To be safe, donate to foreign organizations working in Cambodia that employ Cambodians to run their programs.

Aid Organizations

Tips for Traveling in Cambodia

For a more comfortable and relaxing trip, take time to thoughtfully prepare. The following will give you some good pointers, but you may want to refer to other guidebooks for more extensive travel advice.

Health Advisory

Refer to the Center for Disease Control government website www.cdc.gov for background information and advice. Make an appointment with an international travel doctor, or County Health Department for precautions and immunizations. If possible, start this process several months before your trip as some inoculations need to be spaced months apart. They usually advise that your childhood immunizations be up to date, such as polio, diphtheria and tetanus. For Cambodia, typhoid and hepatitis vaccinations are usually advised. Your doctor will help you decide what to do to prevent malaria. Take and use mosquito repellent because malaria and dengue fever are carried by mosquitoes.

Food

Most health problems come from unclean water. Always drink boiled or bottled water, which are readily available, or purify your own water with iodine. Eat cooked food - not salads or fruit, unless you peel it, or it was prepared in a restaurant that caters to Westerners and uses clean water to wash the fruits and vegetables. Don't buy food on the street or in the open market (flies spread diseases).

Crime and Safety

Check the US State Department website www.state.gov and look under International Travel/Cambodia to learn about current safety precautions. The main problem in Cambodia is purse snatching. Wear your bag with the strap diagonally across your body or use a fanny pack. Keep valuables in a money belt underneath your clothing. Walking alone after dark is not advisable. Driving after dark in rural areas is dangerous as cattle sometimes walk in front of cars.

Photographs

It is polite to ask people's permission before you take their photo. Cambodians are usually happy to please you. A seasoned traveler shared: *"I like to take an old-fashioned Polaroid camera with me, so when I meet new friends and want to take their picture, I can give them a photo to keep. They really appreciate that."*

Dealing with Beggars

This will probably one of the most challenging parts of your trip. The first rule is NEVER give to begging children, because children who make a living on the streets usually end up in drugs, crime, or prostitution. Instead, give to an organization that helps children. Disabled people often find it difficult to make a living. However, we recommend giving to organizations that empower disabled people to help themselves through vocational training. Frequently, beggars are forced to beg by someone else who keeps the money.

Currency

US dollars is the preferred currency in Cambodia. Often, marked up, worn or torn bills are not accepted, so bringing clean, crisp, $1 and $5 bills can make transactions easier for you. The local currency is called riel and is used for change. A 1000 riel bill

equals about 25 cents. Only higher end shops, restaurants and hotels take credit cards. There are ATM machines in the major cities, although they do not always work, so you may need to go to a bank to change traveler's checks into dollars or get a cash advance on a credit card.

Bargaining

The prices in shops are a set price. The vendors in the market will bargain with you. The best strategy is to find out the fair price ahead of time by asking your guide. Then you can bargain down to a price that is fair to you and the seller. Please remember that Cambodians earn very little and if they have not made any sales that day, they may be willing to accept a below-cost offer, just to have money to buy food. Be considerate when you bargain – a dollar is not much to us but it can be a lot to a seller.

When to Go and What to Pack

It is always hot in Cambodia, but the cooler period is November through February. The rainy season is June through October and the very hottest month is April. Travel light. Don't wear expensive jewelry. Wear a money belt. Bring sunscreen, a hat and mosquito repellant.

Travel Companies

There are many companies that offer responsible tours. The companies that we recommend have offices in Cambodia.

About Asia

www.aboutasiatravel.com

Practicing responsible tourism. About Asia's goal is to enrich the lives of customers, employees and the children of Cambodia through the provision of high quality services to visitors to Cambodia. Half of their profits go to charitable foundations focused on the neediest children of Cambodia: orphans, street children and those from families so poor they have no chance of an education. In 2006, they built the first secondary school in rural Siem Reap province.

Carpe Diem Travel Limited

www.carpe-diem-travel.com

An opportunity to learn about other cultures and their way of life. Itineraries are designed to give you time to appreciate your destination. A portion of their profits are reinvested into projects that help local people realise their potential, build their future and improve their environment.

Journeys Within Tour Company

www.journeys-within.com

Described by *Condé Nast Magazine* as "pioneers in philanthropic travel," Journeys Within believes not just in empowering the local people to better their own lives, but in empowering travelers to help give them that chance. Their projects include school sponsorships, water filters and a microfinance program.

PEPY Tours (Protect the Earth, Protect Yourself)

www.pepyride.org

Providing adventure and volunteer travel opportunities in developing areas and also funding the initiatives of grassroots partner organizations in education, the environment and health. Travel with PEPY Tours and "Go where your money goes" by visiting the programs your fundraising efforts support.

See Cambodia Differently

www.seecambodiadifferently.com

A socially-responsible tour company whose policies care for people and the environment. Tours focus on birding, wildlife, yoga, wellness and photography as well as general sightseeing. The company can also arrange cooking classes, cyclo tours, jungle trekking, horse-riding, mountain biking excursions and scuba diving trips.

Further Reading

Cambodia Ancient and Modern History

- *Angkor and the Khmer Civilization (Ancient Peoples and Places)* by Michael D. Coe 2005. Khmer cultural history from the Stone Age through the French Protectorate in 1863.

- *A History of Cambodia* by David P. Chandler 2007 Fourth Edition. A clear and concise comprehensive overview.

- *Soul Survivors – Stories of Women and Children in Cambodia* by Bhavia C. Wagner 2008. Fourteen genocide survivors tell their powerful stories of loss and recovery.

- *Cambodia's Curse: The Modern History of a Troubled Land* by Joel Brinkley 2012.Pulitzer Prize reporter illuminates the deep historical roots of Cambodians' modern-day behavior.

- *Forest of Struggle: Moralities of Remembrance in Upland Cambodia* by Eve Zucker 2013. Restoring social and moral order in a Cambodian village following years of war and conflict.

- *30 Years of Hun Sen: Violence, Repression, and Corruption in Cambodia* by Human Rights Watch 2015.

- *The Killing Fields* DVD Winner of 3 Academy Awards. The true story of a New York Times reporter and his aide caught in the Khmer Rouge genocide in 1975.

Culture

- *Cambodia - Culture Smart!: The Essential Guide to Customs & Culture* by Graham Saunders 2008.

- *Cambodian Cooking: A humanitarian project in collaboration with Act for Cambodia* by Joannes Riviere 2017 From the French NGO that runs Sala Bai Restaurant and cooking school for disadvantaged youth in Siem Reap.

- *Cambodian Dance: Celebration of the Gods* by Denise Heywood 2009.

Responsible Tourism

The Ethical Travel Guide: Your Passport to Exciting Alternative Holidays by Polly Pattullo 2009 Second Edition.

Volunteer: A Traveler's Guide to Making a Difference Around the World by Charlotte Hindle 2007.

Online Resources

News and information www.cambodia.org and www.phnompenhpost.com

Contributing Writers

Tom Auciello is an Engineer who has spent his career in the medical electronics and super computing industries. He currently spends much of his time volunteering and traveling throughout the world.

Kathie Carpenter is Director of Undergraduate Studies for the University of Oregon International Studies Department. She teaches courses on Khmer cinema and development and social change in Cambodia.

Lowell Hill is retired from a technical career. He has visited Cambodia twice, and expects to go again because he thinks the people are wonderful and they and the country are worth helping.

Shoshana Kerewsky is a psychologist and educator in the University of Oregon Counseling Psychology and Human Services Department. She has visited Cambodia several times and has lectured in the Psychology Department of the Royal University of Phnom Penh.

Pujita Nanette Mayeda devotes her time to assisting non-profits with fundraising, consulting, and service projects. She works for Community Supported Shelters, providing non-traditional, transitional shelter to support those experiencing homelessness.

Bhavia Wagner enjoys helping those in need. She is the founder and director of Friendship with Cambodia, a non-profit organization that supports humanitarian projects in Cambodia.

Photo Credits

Vern Arne *Landmine museum, page 43*
Tim Crockett *Earthwalkers, page 33*
David Davis *Tonle Sap Boats, page 44*
Valentina DuBasky *Lieng, page 70, 77*
Carol Gleason *Butterfly, page 37*
Mark Goddard *Monk at Bayon, page xi*
Leeuwtje *Wat Lanka, page 10*
Don Lyon *Apsara, Ta Prohm, Skulls, Lake, page x, xi, xii, xiii*
Pujita Mayeda *Peace Girl, Banteay Srey, Hotels and Restaurants, page xi, xii, 19, 22, 24, 27, 32, 47, 50, 85, 90, back cover*
Heicl Neumeyer *Kampot Sunset, page 53*
Takayuki Senzaki *Angkor Thom, page 29*
Taolmar *Dancer, page 65*
Keith J Smith *Sihanoukville Beach, page x*

Cover & Book Design

**Jennifer Andrews,
Helios Creative, LLC.**
www.helioscreative.com

Further Reading

CPSIA information can be obtained
at www.ICGtesting.com
Printed in the USA
LVOW02s2244110517

534207LV00003B/3/P